Benjamin Watson is one of the most intelligent and thoughtful men I have ever met, inside or outside of football. When he examines a topic, it is never from the perspective of societal norms or cultural traditions. His observations are always based on sound, biblical principles. I know you will benefit from his insights into race and religion in the United States today.

TONY DUNGY
Super Bowl-winning head coach and *New York Times* bestselling author

Packed with germane insights, this eye-opening book challenges current trends in American race relations, providing an important context for conversations about finding roads to racial unity. Read this book and be better prepared to narrow the gap between our national creeds and deeds.

BARRY C. BLACK
Chaplain of the United States Senate

Not many people can speak so honestly and eloquently about such a tough issue. From personal experiences and wisdom, Benjamin Watson shows great perspective on every side and challenges us all to embrace a higher moral and spiritual purpose in solving it.

DREW BREES
Quarterback, New Orleans Saints

If you thought you were moved by Benjamin's words in the wake of Ferguson, wait until you read this book. It is intensely personal, provoking real race discussions based on his own life and the issues still plaguing this nation. More importantly, though, my friend Benjamin leaves us with a sense of hope.

BROOKE BALDWIN
Anchor, CNN

Benjamin Watson is an important African American voice of balance and sanity in a world of racial chaos and confusion. He has used his platform as an NFL player to speak God's perspective on race. In this work, Ben will encourage and challenge you to think rightly and righteously about addressing the sin that is destroying our nation.

DR. TONY EVANS
Senior pastor of Oak Cliff Bible Fellowship and president
of The Urban Alternative

A must-read for anyone who is frustrated by the racial strife and problems in our world—and ready to become part of the solution. Stop everything you're doing and read what Benjamin Watson has to say.

MARK RICHT
Head football coach, University of Georgia

I am honored to recommend my friend Benjamin Watson's first book, *Under Our Skin*. Ben has grabbed the attention of our nation with insightful writings on many of the issues that divide us. God has expanded Ben's reach way beyond the football field. I believe Ben is a voice for our time. In *Under Our Skin*, you will soon see why his wisdom on the issue of race in our nation is so needed.

CHRIS TOMLIN
Musician, songwriter

This is a message every one of us needs to hear, and we're listening to what Benjamin Watson has to say. *Under Our Skin* is unflinchingly honest, strong, and authentic. You won't be able to put it down, and it will surprise, challenge, and inspire you in ways you never expected.

HOLLY ROBINSON PEETE
Actress, author, philanthropist

RODNEY PEETE
Former NFL quarterback, author, entrepreneur

UNDER OUR SKIN

UNDER OUR SKIN

GETTING REAL
ABOUT RACE—
AND GETTING FREE
FROM THE FEARS
AND FRUSTRATIONS
THAT DIVIDE US

BENJAMIN WATSON
WITH KEN PETERSEN

TYNDALE®
MOMENTUM

An Imprint of
Tyndale House Publishers, Inc.

Visit Tyndale Momentum online at www.tyndalemomentum.com.

Tyndale Momentum and the Tyndale Momentum logo are trademarks of Tyndale House Publishers, Inc. Tyndale Momentum is an imprint of Tyndale House Publishers, Inc.

Under Our Skin: Getting Real about Race—and Getting Free from the Fears and Frustrations that Divide Us

Designed by Alberto C. Navata Jr.

Edited by Dave Lindstedt

Published in association with the literary agency of Legacy, LLC, 501 N. Orlando Avenue, Suite #313-348, Winter Park, FL 32789.

ISBN 978-1-4964-1329-1

Printed in the United States of America

21 20 19 18 17 16 15
7   6   5   4   3   2   1

To my mother and father, for teaching me the power of words, to think before I react, to stand firm in my beliefs, and to always speak the truth in love.

CONTENTS

INTRODUCTION

ON AUGUST 9, 2014, I turned on the television in my hotel room at The Greenbrier in White Sulphur Springs, West Virginia, where I was at training camp with my team, the New Orleans Saints. I remember thinking, *No, not again!* as I watched the news reports about how Michael Brown, an unarmed black teenager, had been shot and killed by Darren Wilson, a white police officer, in Ferguson, a suburb of St. Louis, Missouri.

Riots ensued and continued over the next several weeks as every news outlet in America descended on Ferguson during a summer when things seemed to be falling apart and no one could make sense of what was happening. Considering that Eric Garner had died in a police chokehold on the streets of Staten Island only a month earlier, and John Crawford had been shot to death by the police while shopping in an Ohio Walmart on August 5, the national consciousness was on high alert and ready to erupt when word came of yet another questionable death of a black man at the hands of the police.

As protests, mostly peaceful, sprouted up in cities across the country, the outcry against police brutality, coupled with looting and civil unrest, prompted my father to say that he hadn't seen scenes like these since the upheaval of the 1960s. Things had gotten scary, and all the facts had not yet been released or even discovered.

On August 20, a grand jury began hearing evidence to decide whether there was probable cause to indict Darren Wilson for shooting Michael Brown. Over the next three months, eyewitness accounts and testimony from the hearings were leaked to the media, increasing speculation about what the grand jury would decide. *State of Missouri v. Darren Wilson* was often the number one story on the major news networks, with constant updates for each sliver of fact or opinion from a plethora of contributing lawyers, law enforcement officials, and civil rights activists. As week 1 of the NFL season turned into weeks 4, 5, and 6, anticipation mounted. Finally, by mid-November, week 12, we all got our answer.

It was a big week in the Saints' locker room. After stumbling out of the gate, we were a dismal 4–6 and in desperate need of a home win after two straight losses. Our chance to turn things around would come on November 24, on *Monday Night Football*, against a solid Baltimore Ravens team.

As the week progressed and we prepared for the game, there was talk on the networks that an announcement about Ferguson was imminent; but as game time approached, I laid aside my apprehension about when that might happen to focus on the job at hand.

Though the Saints had fared well in night games in recent years, that Monday night game was not one of them, and we were beaten by the Ravens, 34–27. Disappointed about the game and the season in general, I didn't check social media after the game. And because *Monday Night Football* games are broadcast in prime time, they're usually not over until after 11 p.m. anyway. That night, all I wanted to do was meet my wife in the family area and go home.

It was Kirsten who broke the news to me about Ferguson.

"They made a decision," she said, and by the look on her face I could tell it wasn't good. As we made the short drive from the Superdome to our house, she filled me in on the details and on the explosion of response on social media.

When we got home, I stayed up until the early hours of the morning watching the tears, screams, anger, and frustration of people across the nation as they flocked to the streets of their cities. I listened to the legal experts give their opinions and analysis regarding what the grand jury must have seen and heard—or not seen or heard—that led them to determine there was no probable cause to indict Officer Wilson.

After three months of waiting and wondering, I was shocked. I was upset. I was disappointed. I wanted to scream and cry at the same time. It wasn't just about Michael Brown; it was about an entire summer filled with questionable encounters in which black men had lost their lives.

Sometimes, God lays something on my heart, and I have the urge to write. I had that feeling that night, and I tried to organize my thoughts; but I didn't know where to start. Everything I wrote felt as if it didn't quite capture the message I wanted to convey. I was angry, but I didn't want to respond emotionally and later regret what I had said. I went to sleep thinking about how—and even *if*—I should say what I was feeling in my heart.

The next morning, I decided to simply start writing exactly what I was feeling. We were off on Tuesday, as is customary in the NFL, and I didn't have to be back to work until early Wednesday morning. A teammate was hosting an event for the homeless that evening, so between family time with the kids and attending the charity event, my opportunities to write were sporadic.

Later that evening, we stopped at Target to pick up a few household items for a couple who had fallen on hard times. I sat in the car with the kids while my wife went into the store. With my iPhone in hand, I put the finishing touches on the thoughts I had been typing throughout the day in my Notes app.

When I was done, I hesitated for a moment and thought about the response I would receive for engaging in such a divisive situation. Though I'm not proud to admit it, I even second-guessed whether I should mention the hope I have in God, even though it is truly the anchor for my life.

People always say, "*Think* before you push Send." Well, I thought, and then I pushed Send, forwarding my response to a friend who helps with my website so that he could post it to my Facebook account (which, at the time, I had no idea how to do myself). Sitting in the driver's seat, with our four kids behind me, I sent the following post.

At some point while I was playing or preparing to play on *Monday Night Football*, the news broke about the Ferguson decision. After trying to figure out how I felt, I decided to write it down. Here are my thoughts:

I'M ANGRY because the stories of injustice that have been passed down for generations seem to be continuing before our very eyes.

I'M FRUSTRATED because pop culture, music, and movies glorify these types of police-citizen altercations and promote an invincible attitude that continues to get young men killed in real life, away from the safety of movie sets and music studios.

I'M FEARFUL because in the back of my mind I know that although I'm a law-abiding citizen I could still be looked upon as a "threat" to those who don't know me.

So I will continue to have to go the extra mile to earn the benefit of the doubt.

I'M EMBARRASSED because the looting, violent protests, and law breaking only confirm, and in the minds of many, validate, the stereotypes and thus the inferior treatment.

I'M SAD because another young life was lost from his family; the racial divide has widened; a community is in shambles; accusations, insensitivity, hurt, and hatred are boiling over, and we may never know the truth about what happened that day.

I'M SYMPATHETIC because I wasn't there so I don't know exactly what happened. Maybe Darren Wilson acted within his rights and duty as an officer of the law and killed Michael Brown in self-defense like any of us would in the circumstance. Now he has to fear the backlash against himself and his loved ones when he was only doing his job. What a horrible thing to endure. Or maybe he provoked Michael and ignited the series of events that led to his eventually murdering the young man to prove a point.

I'M OFFENDED because of the insulting comments I've seen that are not only insensitive but dismissive to the painful experiences of others.

I'M CONFUSED because I don't know why it's so hard to obey a policeman. You will not win!!! And I don't know why some policemen abuse their power. Power is a responsibility, not a weapon to brandish and lord over the populace.

I'M INTROSPECTIVE because sometimes I want to take "our" side without looking at the facts in situations like these. Sometimes I feel like it's us against them. Sometimes I'm just as prejudiced as people I point fingers at. And that's not right. How can I look at white skin and make assumptions but not want assumptions made about me? That's not right.

I'M HOPELESS because I've lived long enough to expect things like this to continue to happen. I'm not surprised and at some point my little children are going to inherit the weight of being a minority and all that it entails.

I'M HOPEFUL because I know that while we still have race issues in America, we enjoy a much different normal than those of our parents and grandparents. I see it in my personal relationships with teammates, friends, and mentors. And it's a beautiful thing.

I'M ENCOURAGED because ultimately the problem is not a SKIN problem, it is a SIN problem. SIN is the reason we rebel against authority. SIN is the reason we abuse our authority. SIN is the reason we are racist, prejudiced, and lie to cover for our own. SIN is the reason we riot, loot, and burn. BUT I'M ENCOURAGED because God has provided a solution for sin through his son, Jesus, and with it, a transformed heart and mind. One that's capable of looking past the outward and seeing what's truly important in every human being. The cure for the Michael Brown, Trayvon Martin, Tamir Rice and Eric Garner tragedies is not education or exposure. It's the gospel. So, finally, I'M ENCOURAGED because the gospel gives mankind hope.

Within an hour, my wife asked me if I had posted something, because her Facebook was going crazy. Since I wasn't an active Facebook user, I had no idea what was happening online.

Over the next days and weeks, my post was "liked" more than 800,000 times, and I was asked to comment on our struggles with race in America on many major networks and talk shows.

In the locker room, many teammates, coaches, and staff members said, "That's what I was thinking; I just didn't know how to say it." Lines of communication began to open about this tough topic.

I wish I could have read all the comments on Facebook. Most of the ones I saw were quite moving. Many people talked about the tears running down their faces, and the pain they have felt because of racial tensions in our nation. Police officers—including one from St. Louis who contacted me—thanked me for acknowledging their side of the story. Even some celebrities shared my post on their pages, and players from other teams mentioned it on the field after games.

I was invited to speak in churches to urge congregations to address the issue of racism. And most important to me, my wife told me she was proud of me.

I didn't know what would happen when I wrote down my thoughts, but God saw it as fit to reach a multitude of people. If it opened their eyes, their hearts, and their minds in even the smallest way, I'm honored to have helped to narrow the racial divide, even for a moment.

This book, now, is an expansion of my thoughts about these serious and troubling issues. I'm writing not because I have all the answers, but because I have a lot of questions and concerns about how we as Americans with different skin tones relate to one another.

Ferguson was a crucible, where long-simmering tensions

boiled over. Though as black people and white people in twenty-first-century America, we share space and time, Ferguson and other similar situations have shown us how we view the world in totally different ways.

I'm writing because we need to have an open national dialogue about the hot-button issues of race that affect us all. I hope this book will challenge people to have serious, healthy discussions about race and racism. I hope this book will encourage people of all races to have these discussions without fear of saying the wrong thing, insulting others, or being condemned by people who don't agree. The time has come to peel back the layers of our own attitudes and beliefs about race and to be honest with ourselves about our issues when it comes to race. Only then will we experience the change we desperately need.

I am confident that you will agree with some of the things I've written in the book. I'm equally confident that you will oppose, or see differently, other issues I have written about from my personal perspective.

Part of my purpose is to address the emotions that I, and countless others, felt that night when the grand jury decision was announced—emotions that we continue to feel every time the issue of race is brought into the equation. I've changed the order of my original Facebook post, and I combined a couple of entries to allow the manuscript to flow more smoothly; but the message is the same.

My wife and I recently welcomed our fifth child into the world. During one of her doctor visits, I had to fill out some paperwork about myself. I wrote down my name, date of birth, and occupation without hesitation. But when I got to *race* and was asked to check the appropriate box, the options all seemed loaded. Each one immediately conjured up positive or negative images in my head. Some didn't even make sense if you really thought about it. For the first time on a form like that, I selected "other." Not because I'm not proud of my skin color, my ancestry, or my heritage, because I am. I checked "other" because I know that the real humanity, the soul and spirit under our skin, is what makes us who we are.

And on the blank line next to "other," I wrote *HUMAN*.

ANGRY

I'M ANGRY
because the stories of injustice that have been passed down
for generations seem to be continuing before our very eyes.

EVERY YEAR, my parents took us kids to see our grandfather in Washington, DC.

I always loved going to visit Pop Pop, who was my mother's father. He lived on the eleventh floor of a high-rise apartment building near the Watergate Hotel, and we'd walk out onto his balcony to see the lights and sights of the nation's capital. To the right, we could see the Kennedy Center. Straight ahead was the Potomac River. And if we looked left, we had a clear view across the plaza of the Washington Monument. To me, even as a kid, it was breathtakingly beautiful—a solitary spire connecting earth to heaven. Every time we visited, I couldn't wait to gaze on it once again.

Pop Pop's place was filled with what I call old-people trinkets—knickknacks, figurines, little statues, and all sorts of souvenirs—that Pop Pop had picked up here and there throughout his life. For us kids, these constituted a kind of toy store: rows of interesting objects that we could take down, play with on the rug in the living room, and use to create worlds and armies and stories about the lives of make-believe people. Hours of fun. I'm not sure whether we ever realized to what extent these "toys" represented real memories of the years through which Pop Pop had actually lived.

My grandfather was born in 1920. *His* grandfather was born in 1860, at the beginning of the Civil War, into an America where slavery had yet to be abolished. And so, as I have sometimes thought about it, I dodged slavery by just five generations.

To some, that's a long time. Then again, it really wasn't that long ago. Pop Pop lived right in the middle of that not-such-a-long-time between slavery and me.

[My grandfather's] grandfather was born in 1860. . . . As I have sometimes thought about it, I dodged slavery by just five generations.

He grew up in Culpeper, Virginia—only seventy miles from DC, but light-years away in terms of racial attitudes. The limitations that were placed on blacks didn't set well with him, even when he was a young boy. Like many kids, he was just a bit rebellious, but a lot of white people might have called him a delinquent. One hot summer, at the age of thirteen, he decided to jump into the public swimming pool, which of course was designated as whites-only. He went ahead and swam in it anyway. Later, his father got a call from the authorities, who demanded that the family pay for the cost of draining the pool and refilling it with "pure" water.

Before my grandfather reached his midteens, he moved from Culpeper to DC. His parents didn't believe he'd live to see his twenties if they stayed in Culpeper, where, on Saturday nights, Pop Pop was able to see burning crosses in the distance—white people "having fun" on the weekend with their own brand of terrorism.

A full six decades after the abolition of slavery, Pop Pop's world still had separate toilets and drinking fountains for blacks and whites, a distinction validated by the "separate but equal" standard approved by the US Supreme Court in 1896 in its landmark *Plessy v. Ferguson* decision. And as Pop Pop became an adult, he faced limitations in the working world as well. He often told me that I could do whatever I set my mind on doing. "But," he cautioned, "understand that because you're black, there's always a ceiling. You can go only so far up the totem pole."

He ran into that ceiling often enough in his life, I think, but he didn't seem to let it stop him. He served his country for several years in the army, and though he never was sent overseas, he put in his time as a supply officer and was honorably discharged. Later, he got a job as a pressman in the Government Printing Office, which became his main employment for much of his life until he retired in 1976. He also maintained a side job as a bartender, working at an officer's club in town and catering various events.

Pop Pop took pride in himself. He was five foot seven, slender, and always well dressed. He wore a handsome Kangol hat, which was a variation on a beret but with a wider brim. I think people back then dressed better than we do today, but Pop Pop especially cared about his appearance. That went for his apartment, too. He kept it meticulously clean—to this day, when I smell Listerine I think of the antiseptic smell of his place—and he maintained everything in neat order, with all his old-people trinkets lined up and in their places. It was as if he had a plan for his life, was living it out, and was tracking his progress on the shelves in his apartment.

He was popular. I remember him always knowing a lot of people while I was growing up. He was very social. Many people along the street would acknowledge him by name as he walked by. He had lived in Washington most of his life and had accumulated friends for a long time. People—black and white—loved him.

For all the social limitations faced by a black man in the 1940s and '50s, Pop Pop had made a good life for himself.

For all the social limitations faced by a black man in the 1940s and '50s, Pop Pop had made a good life for himself. If there was a ceiling for a black person, so be it; Pop Pop seemed intent on making sure his life filled as much of the space under that ceiling as it possibly could.

Pop Pop had several passions. One was golf. He loved play-ing the game. Some of the little statues he kept at home were of golfers positioned in various stages of their swing. He also had golf balls lying around his place. As a kid, I thought about taking one of his Champion golf balls, going out onto the balcony, and throwing it as far as I could toward the Washington Monument. Later in life, Pop Pop gave me a set of golf clubs, hoping perhaps that I'd become a golfer like him. But it never took. I pursued this other thing instead—football.

Pop Pop's second passion was Cadillacs. Black people weren't supposed to be able to afford one, and that may have been the source of his passion. He owned a forest-green Caddy and was extremely proud of it. He had a lead foot and always drove fast—because he *could* in that thing. He would take us to Safeway, and it was so much fun to sit in the back seat of the Caddy (with-out seatbelts) and slide back and forth while he drove fast and took hard turns. Dangerous, maybe, but loads of fun. And we all survived, with glee, what was otherwise just a simple trip to the grocery store.

Finally, Pop Pop had one other passion: dental floss.

When he turned fifty, Pop Pop got braces. It certainly wasn't pleasant for him, coming so late in his life, but after the braces were taken off, he developed a new appreciation for good teeth. Part of his daily tooth-care obsession involved the near-constant use of dental floss. He was always flossing.

Sometimes he actually fell asleep with floss still in his mouth. When he'd nod off like that, sometimes there would be a single string of floss hanging out over his lip and down to his chin.

When my sister, Jessica, and I saw him asleep like this, we'd giggle. Sometimes, we'd quietly walk up to him and get really close to his face, and one of us would carefully put a finger close to his mouth to touch the hanging strand of floss. It would move, and we'd stop, trying not to laugh and hoping it wouldn't wake him up. It wouldn't, and we'd get bolder, actually taking the hanging strand of floss between our fingers and starting to pull it. We always thought that maybe sometime we could slowly pull the whole strand of floss out of his mouth without waking him up. But we never went that far, always chickening out at the last minute.

Even today when I think of Pop Pop, I smile a lot, and I laugh at some of the memories.

But I remember other things as well. He didn't often reveal it to me because I was just a kid, but he was angry about the racism he'd encountered as a child, as a young man, and as a proud black man in the prime of his life. He didn't usually express his social activism to me, but he would talk to my mom and other adults in the family. I think I could sense it, though, around the edges of his smile, his playfulness with us kids, and his immense joy in the simple passions of life. There was hurt and anger there.

It makes me wonder.

I wonder about this dapper man in a Kangol hat who made a lot out of himself despite the limits society imposed on him. I wonder why he so often said to me, "When you're black, there's always a ceiling." Was it because he knew he was living a life destined for limitations and he was just making the most of it?

Were his words a challenge to me, or were they a warning? . . . Was he calling me to step up and overcome the obstacles, just as he had?

When he said, "You can go only so far up the totem pole," were his words a challenge to me, or were they a warning? Did he want me to know that even today I don't have the same opportunities as white people? Or was he calling me to step up and overcome the obstacles, just as he had?

Isn't that the real dilemma of the race problem?

What was the message of Pop Pop's life? Was it all of the above?

I wonder.

And I wonder why the Washington Monument seems to stretch only halfway up for black people. Why is it that, even today, in the United States of America, we as a race are so often kept from touching the sky?

． ． ．

I'm angry because white people don't get it.

I'm angry because black people don't get it, either.

And now that I've ticked off everyone equally, let me say my piece.

Five generations and 150 years have passed since the abolition of slavery.

I'm angry because white people don't get it. I'm angry because black people don't get it, either.

You'd think that after all this time we'd have reached real parity between the races, that there would be *truly* equal opportunity, and that we'd be seeing and experiencing fairness in society between blacks and whites.

A lot of white people believe that's actually where we are. A lot of black people know we aren't.

Certainly by the time of Pop Pop's life—smack dab in the middle between slavery and the present—you'd think there would have been a lot of social progress, a shaking out of the issues and biases, and a lessening of racial conflicts. If you pinpointed a specific year of his adult life—let's say when he was thirty-five, some *ninety years* after the abolition of slavery—you'd think we as a nation would have reached some level of equality and social fairness between blacks and whites.

But Pop Pop's thirty-fifth birthday was September 24, 1955. Rosa Parks had not yet refused to give up her seat on the bus in Montgomery, Alabama. That wouldn't happen for another two months. Ninety years after slavery, blacks were still segregated from whites. They still had separate drinking fountains, separate restrooms, separate neighborhoods, and separate schools. They still were expected to sit at the back of the bus.

Ninety years is a long time. And yet not such a long time.

And here's what many people don't really understand.

Though the Thirteenth Amendment abolished slavery in the post–Civil War union, it really didn't end it. A new era of slavery—or as Douglas Blackmon so poignantly describes it, an "age of neoslavery"—had begun.[1] This became an age of human trafficking, forced labor, Black Codes, Jim Crow, and the ever-present terror of white supremacist groups like the Ku Klux Klan.

This was not freedom.

Rather than milk and honey, the Promised Land for many black Americans was filled with more blood, more tears, and more repression. And so, ninety years after abolition, Rosa Parks was still required to sit in the back of the bus.

Much of my anger arises from the largely untold stories of men and women who faced a legal system that arrested, tried, and sentenced them for crimes they did not commit (if they were fortunate enough to even have a trial). I come to a slow boil when I watch documentaries or read memoirs about these post-slavery generations whose lives have been largely disregarded in history books.

There's a feeling in white America that everything is equal now. But black people know in their bones that there's still a residue of neoslavery that sticks to so much of life.

Yes, today, 150 years after slavery, it's true that we're not as segregated as black people were in Pop Pop's day. But perhaps I should say "not segregated *in the same way*."

Black people still are limited by the quality of schools they're able to attend. Black people are often grouped into segregated voting districts.[2] A disproportionate number of black people are rotting away in prison, its own form of segregation.

It's true that we're not as segregated as black people were in Pop Pop's day. But perhaps I should say "not segregated *in the same way.*"

"Twenty-first-century segregation exists overtly in our school systems, communities, and prisons," writes Reniqua Allen in *The Guardian*. "It also permeates our society in ways we don't even realize."[3]

Many today might agree that a lot of official segregation has been eliminated (though some would quarrel even with that), but certainly segregation is still here, embedded in social systems, cultural biases, and prejudice. In an article in *The Atlantic* titled, "Is Racial Segregation Legal, If It's Not Deliberate?" Garrett Epps writes, "The sunny, 'look how far we've come' view seems particularly hard to justify in housing. Anyone who can look at American cities—their housing patterns, their employment figures, or their police policies—and see a new dawn of color blindness is wearing glasses unavailable to me."[4]

And then there's church. The church, I believe, has the greatest opportunity to effect change in our communities. Yet it remains the most segregated institution in America. *Christianity Today* reported in January 2015 that "Sunday morning remains one of the most segregated hours in American life, with more than 8 in 10 congregations made up of one predominant racial group."[5]

I'm angry that so many still try to argue against the truth of these basic facts.

Some say that blacks themselves choose some forms of segregation, preferring to live and worship among themselves in their own communities and their own churches. Some of that may be true, though research indicates that black people are much more inclined toward diversity than white people are.[6] Whatever the case, the point is unchanged.

We're still segregated.

Some say that there is a disproportionate incarceration rate for blacks because blacks are more likely to commit crimes than whites. It's hard not to interpret that assumption as inherently racist, but either way we still must account for the fact that there are *six times* as many black people incarcerated as white people.[7] Really? You mean there's nothing in that number to even remotely suggest that blacks are disproportionately targeted and arrested?

But again, regardless of the argument, *we're still segregated.*

Not many people would suggest that education isn't a serious problem; however, some have argued that it's such a complex problem that nothing can be done about it. I agree that it's complex, but many also say that nothing *ought* to be done—that it's a "poverty problem," a "money problem," or a "ghetto problem," and that any effort to change the status quo would disadvantage people who are wealthier.

And while people argue, *we're still segregated.*

I'm also angry that this has become about one side or the other winning an argument. Therein lies another hidden attitude toward the race problem. Why is this about winning and losing? Doesn't anyone else see that *we're all losing?*

Why don't we get it? Why can't we grasp the truth that, by separating ourselves as whites and blacks, we are so much less likely to understand one another, show compassion, and prevent violence?

Why can't we get past the talking points of the debate and see clearly the young boy who was shot, the mother who tragically lost her son, and the confusion and fear of the cops involved—some of whom, too, were black?

Why can't we drop the posturing, the media skirmishes, and the shouting arguments and do something about this? If not for our own sake, then at least for our kids'?

A hundred and fifty years is a long time—and yet, apparently, not such a long time.

.   .   .

Then there's the quiet echo of Pop Pop's life.

His life says, "Make the most of what you have."

It says, "Be proud of who you are."

It says, "Don't let the obstacles and injustice and unfairness limit you. Overcome them."

Well, I'm angry because too many young people—black *and* white—*live down* to the lower expectations people have of them.

I'm angry because systemic prejudice and bias, though just as real in our time as in Pop Pop's time, have become crutches for young people today and excuses for underachieving.

I'm angry because the brooding hate that paces the streets of a small town is a cowardice that leads nowhere. It's cowardly because you can do better, achieve more, and rise above, but you're afraid to try. It leads nowhere, because it never accomplishes anything—it doesn't lead to pride or respect or opportunity. It just leads to destruction.

I'm angry because this is a negative cycle, a downward spiral. It begins with social situations that seriously disadvantage black people. But the cycle extends and continues because so many black people *settle into* their disadvantage and don't ever rise above it. Why can't more blacks grab the opportunities that *do* exist, rather than gripe about opportunities that don't? And why don't more young black people take hold of what they have and rise above?

> Why can't more blacks grab the opportunities that *do* exist, rather than gripe about opportunities that don't?

Yes, I'm really big on personal responsibility. Sometimes I want to take some of these kids and—well, let's just say I want to give them a real hard talking-to.

I want to say, "Okay, so all this has happened to you and set you back in life. You were born into a race that was victimized by slavery. That legacy follows you even now, and life today isn't fair to you. You started out behind the eight ball.

"But what are you going to do about it?"

I want to say, "You know, a lot of people face serious disadvantages in life. You're not the only one. Some were born with disabilities. Others suffered paralyzing accidents. Still others here and around the world were born into severe poverty, at a level you cannot imagine. You're not the only one to face unfairness and hardship. I can tell you stories of many other young people who chose to *do something* to overcome their circumstances.

"So you don't have everything you'd like. But what are you going to do with what you *do* have?"

I want to say, "I know it's hard. And yeah, I know *they* make it hard for you. But are you afraid of doing the hard thing? What's it going to take for you to step up, step out, and step apart?

"Are you going to be one of the ones to change this generation?"

I want to say, "Search for opportunities to learn—find them, scratch and claw to get them. The question is not, 'Why don't *they* do more for me?' The question is, 'Why don't *you* do more for *yourself*?'

"How are *you* going to get yourself an education? Are you willing to go after it?"

I want to say, "News flash: This is not about what white people do to keep you down. If you live your life in reaction to that, then they *will* keep you down. No, this is about pulling yourself up. Are you willing to rise above?"

Yes, you can overcome and do something good and great. But that's something only *you* can do. No one else can or will do it for you.

I want to say, "What is your vision for yourself? How can you make the most of what you have? What opportunities out there can you grab hold of? Yes, you can overcome and do something good and great. But that's something only *you* can do. No one else can or will do it for you.

"Will you do something great for yourself?"

Yes, I want to say all these things.

I guess I just did.

Sometimes I sound like an echo of Pop Pop's life.

·　■　·

This problem of black and white in our world is not a black-and-white issue.

It's complex. It's not about winning an argument. It's usually not about either/or—"this person should have done this" or "that person should have done that."

It's about *both/and*.

Around noon on August 9, 2014, in Ferguson, Missouri, a white police officer, Darren Wilson, shot an eighteen-year-old black man, Michael Brown.

We know that Brown was unarmed. We also know that, minutes earlier, he had stolen cigarillos from a nearby convenience store. We know that Wilson spotted Brown walking with a friend in the middle of the street. Wilson drove his cruiser in front of the two, and there was an altercation through the window of the car. Two shots were fired. One apparently hit Brown in the hand.

Brown and his friend took off running. The friend hid behind a car. Wilson got out of his car and pursued Brown.

From that point on, reports of the incident conflict with each other. Some say that Brown stopped, turned around, raised his arms, and was shot by Wilson anyway. Others say that Brown never raised his hands, suggesting that Brown's turning to face Wilson was a threatening move.

Wilson fired his gun twelve times. At least six bullets hit Brown, and the last bullet was likely the one that killed him.

In the legal proceedings later, there were anomalies regarding evidence, including the chain of custody of Wilson's gun and the state of Michael Brown's body, which lay at the scene for four hours.

The shooting sparked unrest, protests, and violence in Ferguson.

On November 24, 2014, the St. Louis County grand jury decided not to indict Darren Wilson, citing lack of evidence and suggesting that eyewitnesses supporting Wilson were more credible than those supporting Brown.

The grand jury announcement sparked more unrest in Ferguson . . . and it started anew the national conversation about race and racism.

The grand jury announcement sparked more unrest in Ferguson, more violence, more protests. And it started anew the national conversation about race and racism.

As I write this account of these events, I struggle to tell it based on facts and not opinions. I realize that, at every turn in this sequence of events, there's a pro–Michael Brown version of what went down and a pro–Darren Wilson version. I don't assume that all blacks see it one way and all whites see it the other way, but we know that it splits substantially along those lines. We're all biased, aren't we? So much is based on long-developed and deep-seated racial attitudes—some of which we didn't even realize we had. I understand that *somebody* reading this is likely to argue with whatever I suggest about the events of this tragedy.

Truth is, I really don't know what happened, other than what's been reported. I wasn't there. And even if I had been there, my own version of the events would have been based on what little part of the scene I actually could see, and it might have been twisted by my own biases and by the fact that I didn't have all the information and didn't see everything.

But I'll tell you what I believe. I believe in *both/and*.

I believe that it should be possible for blacks and whites to live together peaceably in the same small town. *And* I believe that any town that is two-thirds black and has a police force that is 94 percent white is more likely to have a race problem that erupts in violence.

> A *both/and* view of events . . . reflects the complexity of the issue. That's why the problem of black and white in our world is not a black-and-white issue.

I believe that it must be very difficult for white cops to maintain order in a predominantly black town without legitimate police work being perceived as racially motivated. *And* I believe it's likely that sometimes police work *is* racially motivated and biased. *Both* can be true.

I believe that white people look at law enforcement and assume it is good, based on their experiences and interactions with the police. *And* I believe that black people look at law enforcement and assume—based on patterns and history and experience—that someone is out to get them. I believe *both* are true.

I believe that Michael Brown committed a theft and ran away

from Darren Wilson. *And* I believe that if a white man had committed the same theft and acted in the same way, he'd probably still be alive today.

I believe we are still segregated. *And* I believe that if we were less segregated, some people would be less likely to run and others less likely to shoot.

I don't say these things in order to straddle the line or avoid the controversy. I truly believe that often there is a *both/and* view of events that reflects the complexity of the issue. That's why the problem of black and white in our world is not a black-and-white issue.

Both/and captures the anger and agony of Ferguson. But this story is not just about Ferguson. It's about America. It's about you and me.

You see, there's one more thing I believe. Though I may not know everything that went down on the streets of Ferguson that day, I know one thing for certain: No one here is innocent. The town is guilty—*and* the cops are guilty. Darren Wilson is guilty—*and* Michael Brown is guilty.

And you and I are *both* guilty.

We all have malice deep down.

We all harbor wrong attitudes toward others.

At its core, the issue is not about race. It's about the human heart.

We can talk forever about desegregation; about what cops are justified in doing or not; about what a young black man should have done or not done; about what a town should do or not do on the front lines of a tragedy. But for all the talking heads, all the online chatter and media churning, this will happen again. It already has. Nothing will change . . . unless . . .

Unless God changes our hearts and minds.

God, hear our prayer . . .

. . .

Anger is okay. The question about anger is, what do you do with it? Do you use it to throw fuel on the fire? Or do you use it to fix the problem? Every angry person, myself included, should ask this self-directed question.

Maybe a more difficult question to ask is whether you can use your anger as a motivation to change yourself. What do you need to do to change your own attitudes? What are the biases and prejudices hidden inside you? What are the blind spots you're not willing to look for?

> I'm talking to white people *and* black people. *Both.* ... Let's use our anger to fix the problem. Let's allow change to happen, starting with ourselves.

I'm talking to white people *and* black people. *Both.* I'm talking to myself. We all need God to change our hearts and minds. So let's use our anger to fix the problem. Let's allow change to happen, starting with ourselves.

Can we do that? Can we talk and listen with open hearts and open minds?

I want to talk about the historical legacy of slavery that black people carry inside themselves today. I want to talk about the indelible images of African slaves, kidnapped and brought to America, that are imprinted in the consciousness of so many black people. I want to talk about the overarching truths that black people today are still not treated as equal to white people and that insidious prejudice and segregation still remain all these years after abolition.

Black and white, are we willing and ready to talk about these things?

I want to talk about personal responsibility. I want to talk about the need to let go of some images and legacies—those parts that fuel anger and violence. I want to talk about the present and the future, and about how we would do well not to dwell so much on past hurts but rather to build for ourselves a new future. I want to talk about the embarrassment of racial violence and about how so many angry responses simply reinforce the stereotypes that many white people have of black people.

Black and white, are we willing and ready to talk about these things?

Most of all, are we—both black people and white—ready to admit when our anger is simply unfounded or a result of our cultural lenses? Can we be honest with ourselves and about ourselves?

The question about anger is, what do we do with it?

Let's do something constructive with it.

■　■　■

Parents just want their children to come home.

I saw an interview with Anderson Cooper and the mothers of Michael Brown, Trayvon Martin, Tamir Rice, and Eric Garner, four black men (or boys in the case of Tamir Rice and Trayvon Martin) killed in confrontations with law enforcement over a period of two and a half years. They talked about some of the things I've been saying—namely, the disparity between how white people and black people perceive these tragedies. They argued about the injustices their sons endured in death. They spoke of how the justice system failed them and their sons.

I happened to glance at the comments section below the video on the website. It listed a number of hateful statements, including these:

"This is not racism; this is justice!"

"These men were all criminals and deserved what they got!"

"If these women had raised their kids better . . ."

My mind went into debate mode, internally arguing with these naysayers and skeptics: the indignant, self-righteous responders who were calling out against what the mothers were saying.

Then I came back to focus on the four women. Now I saw them differently. They were just moms. And the pain in their voices was so evident.

One thing cannot be argued: These mothers lost their sons.

As a black man with black sons and daughters, I'm very aware of the dangers for my kids in a society so divided about race.

As a father of four, I understand at least a little of their pain. As a black man with black sons and daughters, I'm very aware of the dangers for my kids in a society so divided about race. My wife and I will teach them as best we can to make good choices for themselves, to be the most they can be, and to follow God with all their hearts. But as they get older, we don't know exactly where they will go, what steps they will take, and what might happen in this world of black and white that is never quite so black-and-white.

Ultimately, I just want them to be able to come home.

Some years ago, as Kirsten and I started having kids, we took them to meet Pop Pop in Washington, just as my parents had taken me once a year. I remember one time when we had our newborn Grace with us. Pop Pop was holding Grace in his arms. Her still-tiny head rested fully in the palm of his hand. He whispered to her softly, "I carry all my babies just like this. I carried your grandmom just like this. I carried your dad just like this."

You see, in the end we're not white or black. We're families. Each of us is just someone's dad, someone's mom, someone's son or daughter.

And someone's grandchild. As my career flourished, Pop Pop was so proud of me. He would look at me with a smile and say, "So now you're a pro football player." He'd say that, and he'd nod. It was a statement of approval and pride. At some point, he started collecting souvenirs and football cards of the teams I played for. They found the most prestigious spot—alongside the other old-people trinkets on his shelves.

Pop Pop died when he was ninety-three. He passed on six months before Michael Brown was shot.

I don't know what he would've said about Ferguson. He never talked much about social issues with me, maybe because he hoped and prayed I would not be affected by them as he had been. But he expressed his opinions and anger to others. He would have had very strong emotions about Ferguson.

I expect he might have seen himself in the person of Michael Brown. He was thirteen when he moved to Washington, DC. Brown was shot at the age of eighteen. Maybe Pop Pop would've imagined himself—that restless, rebellious young kid in Culpeper—living for five more years in the flickering shadows of those burning crosses. What a different path his life might have taken.

I expect that Pop Pop... would have said to me, "Just remember. Remember us. Remember me. Continue to make us proud. Keep going."

I expect that Pop Pop understood the significance of choosing the right path and building a different and better life.

And I expect that, had he lived to see the events in Ferguson unfold, he would have said to me, "Just remember. Remember us. Remember me. Continue to make us proud. Keep going."

After all the arguments, after all the debates, after all the anger, I think that may be the best advice of all.

Pop Pop, I do remember you. And I will keep going.

■ ■ ■

I saw Pop Pop literally on his deathbed, one week before he died. He looked at me with tired eyes, but even then they had a slight twinkle. With the faintest smile on his face, he said, "So now you're a pro football player."

INTROSPECTIVE

I'M INTROSPECTIVE
*because sometimes I want to take "our" side without
looking at the facts in situations like these . . .*

My wife, Kirsten, and I are sometimes active in a small group. I say "sometimes" because, unfortunately, that's an on-and-off thing, given my schedule. During the football season, it's impossible to be consistently involved in any sort of social group outside of football. But during the off-season, Kirsten and I have more opportunities to get together with friends. Sometimes we find ourselves in a small group. Sometimes we read a book and discuss it together. Sometimes we do a Bible study.

In many ways, I think the small group is the real church. Kirsten and I attend a large nearby church, and we love it there—both the preaching and the worship. It's a great church for our kids, too. But our small group is where we have the closest friendships and most honest conversations.

In June 2015, there was another small group that got together at 7:30 on a Wednesday night. It was a church group like mine that had been meeting for some time to study the Bible. On that particular night, there was a new guy. He sat with the group and entered into conversation about the Bible passage they were studying.

Then, after about an hour, he pulled out a gun and started shooting.

The city was Charleston, South Carolina. The church was Emanuel African Methodist Episcopal Church. The shooter was a young white man named Dylann Roof.

All his victims were black. One was the pastor of the church. We now know the story. Roof, a self-declared white supremacist, harbored deep anger toward black people. He eventually took out his rage by shooting a small group of black church members in a church that, notably, has historic racial significance.

The tragedy unified the nation in the midst of a series of racial incidents that had divided it. For once, here was something whites and blacks could agree on. When such evil is launched against a group of people studying the Bible inside a church, it violates both white and black. It strikes home because it could be any one of us and our friends. If it happened there, it could happen here. If it could happen in a church, then it could easily happen in any public place, or even in our homes.

The tragedy unified the nation in the midst of a series of racial incidents that had divided it. For once, here was something whites and blacks could agree on.

In the aftermath, many whites and blacks, together for once, truly grieved over the loss of life, the pain and suffering in the hearts of the bereaved family members, and the violence done to that church and community.

Later, media pundits and commentators talked a lot about Dylann Roof.

"Here is racism," the media analysts generally said. "Cold, calculated racism—embodied in one young man, Dylann Roof. Here is the problem of racism in our country."

But I don't agree. The problem of racism is *not* Dylann Roof.

Yes, he's a racist. That much is clear from the ugly details of his personal manifesto. And yes, the Charleston shooting is an example of extreme racism. It's easy to denounce. It's easy to point our fingers outward. Though tragic, it may actually make us feel a little better inside because we can point to someone else, someone apart, someone extreme, someone on whom we can hang the sign "Racist." We can say, "There, over there, is racism, and we have to do something about him. Over there." As if the trial and sentencing of Dylann Roof will end racism.

We need to do justice, certainly, and do what needs to be done with Dylann Roof and others like him. But whatever is done with him will not eliminate racism. It won't even make a dent in it. The problem of racism in America is not neatly wrapped up in one Dylann Roof, whom we can easily point to and decry. It's not even in the KKK, as evil as they are. It's not in the pockets of white supremacy groups lurking around the country. The real problem of racism is not in the extremes at the edges of society. The problem of racism is not in "that guy over there."

> **The real problem of racism is not in the extremes at the edges of society. The problem of racism is not in "that guy over there." It's right here.**

It's right here.

I confess to you that the problem of racism is inside *me*.

And I suggest the problem of racism is inside you as well.

. . .

My first friend in school was a white kid named Bert.

We became friends in preschool, went to kindergarten together, and hung out with each other through parts of grade school. There was a time when my family moved away from Norfolk, Virginia, to South Carolina. But some years later, we moved back. When I returned, Bert was still there, and we picked up our friendship where we'd left off.

Bert was tall for his age, lanky even at the age of five. Our friendship was probably the first significant relationship I had with a white kid. And he was really, *really* white. I didn't know back then what nationality his ancestors were, but it had to have been northern European, maybe German. I just knew he descended from some people who liked to go hunting. Bert and his family loved to hunt.

As friends, Bert and I could hardly have been more different. I was black; he was white. I loved athletics; he loved hunting and fishing. He wasn't into sports and didn't have an athletic body. And when he ran, it was plain ugly. He had this strange motion, a kind of loping stride that was awkward and rather humorous. See, Bert had really large feet. And they weren't helpful when it came to running. I figured they must've gripped the ground a lot more than normal feet because, when he ran, it was like he was pulling his legs up out of the mud. It was as if he were dragging a refrigerator, but there was nothing behind him. And yet despite all that, Bert could surprise you with his quickness. His long legs somehow overachieved, and those loping strides would get him to the finish line faster than you'd ever imagine.

Bert's family was the total opposite of mine. They were outdoorsy (boating, fishing, shoot-your-own-dinner). . . . My family was into sports and fixing up old cars.

Bert's family was the total opposite of mine. They were an outdoorsy (boating, fishing, shoot-your-own-dinner) kind of crowd. I didn't know anything about any of that. My family was into sports and fixing up old cars.

One night, Bert's mom invited me to dinner. She served sloppy joes. They were really good, but they didn't taste quite the way I was used to. Not like my mom made. That was okay. Maybe white people had their own recipes.

Later, when Bert and I left the table and went outside to play, he asked me, "What'd ya think of the meal?"

"Was pretty good, I'd say."

"Wasn't made with hamburger meat."

"No?" I was afraid to ask.

"Venison. Deer meat."

Well. I didn't know how I felt about that. It didn't seem quite right to me to eat the flesh of a deer that Bert's dad had shot to death. But I had to admit it was really good—just unusual. I figured I'd have to just think of it as something different, some kind of Daniel Boone stew.

Bert taught me about fishing, among other things. A lot of eastern Virginia is covered with inland waterways, rivers, and marshland. His house backed up to a creek, and his family had a dock. The creek fed into the Lafayette River, and Bert and I would often play at the foot of the river bridge, digging up crabs and mussels. My family wasn't into any of that, so it was Bert who taught me about mussels and crabs—and about crab boils, which are common in Maryland and Virginia.

Most often, we would sit on the end of the dock with our fishing poles baited and cast into the creek, waiting for the fish to bite. Bert was the one who taught me about using minnows for bait. I didn't know what a minnow was until he told me. We'd catch minnows in the stream and use them to catch bigger fish.

Only problem was, there weren't really many fish in the creek. In all those summers when we sat at the end of the dock fishing, I remember us catching only a few. Maybe seven total. And when we did catch one, we just threw it back. When I think back on it now, almost the only things we ever really caught were minnows.

But that was just fine. Bert and I were friends. We were outside, just sitting on a dock and talking. Black and white didn't matter—only the blue skies of summer.

■ ■ ■

I wonder how the seeds of racism get planted in the innocence of a child's heart.

Researchers have found that even preschool children are

aware of racial differences between themselves and others.[1] They can detect differences of color, certainly, but also facial features. The signs of racial awareness may be detectable even in infants at six months.[2] But an awareness of racial difference is a far cry from racist attitudes and assumptions. Most research confirms what we've already figured out on our own: We pick up our attitudes, assumptions, and prejudices from the world around us. We learn how to think and feel toward other races and ethnic groups from our parents, teachers, friends, and neighbors. Our attitudes come from those whom we hang out with. They come from the movies and TV we watch. The music we listen to. The video games we play.

Even preschool children are aware of racial differences. . . . But an awareness of racial difference is a far cry from racist attitudes and assumptions.

And sometimes, a life experience jolts us into the reality of race relations in the world.

One of my other good friends growing up was a white kid named Andy. We both were athletes, competing alongside and against each other in every sport we could play in the schoolyard. Soccer, football, and basketball were our favorites. If an elementary school could have jocks, Andy and I were the ones— the white guy and the black guy playing any and every sport in friendly competition to determine who was better.

One of the girls at our school was Katie—blonde, freckled, and pretty. And she was smart: She could add *and* divide. She was athletic and could whup most of the boys in our class on the soccer field. To a nine-year-old boy like me, Katie was really cute. In fact, Katie was really cute to almost *every* boy in school—she stole a lot of hearts. There were contests on the playground about which of the guys Katie would notice first. I in particular was developing a crush on her. And since I was starting to stand out because of my athleticism, I thought maybe I stood a chance.

Even though I didn't have any money, I found a way to get some chocolates that I hoped to give to Katie at school for Valentine's Day.

We ate lunch in the gym, which was converted each day into a cafeteria with lunch tables and chairs pulled out from the sides. I remember that the school had attached a large electric stoplight to the wall opposite the tables. When the noise in the cafeteria got too loud, the red light would blaze on, which was our cue to shut up. Silence was required for a period of time until the red light was turned off.

On Valentine's Day, Andy and I ate lunch together, along with Akio, who was Japanese. We were together at one of the tables, just talking. All the while I was thinking of how I would give Katie the chocolates I'd bought as a gift.

And then Andy said something that would change my life. "You know," he said, "Katie would like you if you were white."

It was as if someone had dropped a bomb in the middle of the table. I wanted the big red stoplight to go off and for everyone to shut up. I wanted to dial back time to the moments before this vile thing was said so that I could somehow stop it.

This wasn't just about my grade-school crush. It was about my being different and *other*. Though I was aware that I attended a predominantly white school, I had never really looked at it that way. Now, however, I suddenly could see myself—the blackness of my face and body—in the midst of this sea of white people. I was different from them. And because I was different, I wasn't good enough.

The bombshell that Andy launched that day had a "note" attached to it—at least for me. One of my best friends was saying that it was obvious to everyone I was black and that everyone knew that was a difference. And not just a difference but a Difference, a Problematic Difference. It made me suddenly aware that everyone saw me in black-and-white terms. What were others saying about my race that would disqualify me from Katie in everyone's mind? And what else did it disqualify me from?

I suddenly could see myself—the blackness of my face and body—in the midst of this sea of white people. I was different from them.

I wasn't the only schoolboy to go through heartbreak over a girl. But I may have been the only boy at *that* school who went through heartbreak over the realization that my race was—apparently—a problem to everyone else.

It was only later that I came to understand that what I heard that day at lunch was the core message that many black people hear at various times, and in various ways, in their lives:

"You know, you *are* different . . ."

"Unfortunately, you don't qualify . . ."

"You would be liked/accepted/deemed worthy if only you weren't black . . ."

On that day, walking home with a box of melting chocolates, I knew my world had changed. Though I had certainly known before that day that I was black and others were white, it was simply a general observation without judgment or consequence. But now it had become personal and negative. And I realized in a different way what it meant to attend a white school while living in a black neighborhood.

My relationship with Andy changed after that. We still played sports together that year and in years to come, but now it was more competitive, more intense, and more fierce. Now I wanted to *beat* him. In every sport, my goal was to outdo him, to defeat him, to be better than him. Even in the classroom, I wanted to score higher than Andy, and I'd always ask how he did on a test so I could find out if my grade was better.

We were just kids. Fourth graders. And on one unfortunate Valentine's Day, without knowing what was happening, without meaning to do anything wrong, without intending to change our friendship or our world, Andy and I found ourselves on opposite sides.

We became racialized.

. . .

I think young children grow up with an awareness of race but also an acceptance of race. When we're young, our playmates are, to us, simply blond or tall or female or noisy or brown- or peach-skinned. Race is a neutral part of how we understand the world as children. But as we get older we begin to learn from those around us—our parents, our friends, our friends' parents—and we pick up their attitudes about race. Brown and peach become black and white.

> Young children grow up with an awareness of race but also an acceptance of race. . . . Race is a neutral part of how we understand the world.

We each view every event in life through a specific set of lenses. These lenses are crafted from birth, initially affected by our families of origin and subsequently molded by various encounters with the people, paradigms, problems, and places we encounter in life. Race, economics, and religion contribute hugely to shape our worldview; they also bind us into a group identity. And we tend to adopt the attitudes and prejudices of the groups we're in.

In short, at some point in life, perhaps as early as grade school, we find ourselves "taking a side" in the racial debate. We become aware that the differences *matter*.

"Our side" isn't usually a viewpoint that we've researched objectively or studied extensively, or about which we've intentionally weighed the facts. Maybe a few try to do that, but not most of us. We simply hold to a perspective that we feel is right because we've been told (conditioned) to believe it's right. Our group says so. Our family says so. It must be right.

Maybe "our side" comes from the experience of one Valentine's Day, the girl we had a crush on, and the friend who told us the way of the world. Or from the experience of being a friend of Michael Brown, Trayvon Martin, or Eric Garner. Or from the horror experienced by the young niece of Tywanza Sanders. She survived the attack by Dylann Roof in the AME church in Charleston, while her uncle did not.

Yes, many of us have experiences that have shaped the "side" we're on.

So does my white friend Chris.

. . .

Chris and I met not long ago when we became involved in a business venture. We became friends of a sort, somehow able to talk frankly about racial issues even though we often found ourselves on opposite sides.

Chris grew up in a home that gave him positive racial attitudes, but in adulthood his perspective changed.

Chris grew up in a home that gave him positive racial attitudes, but in adulthood his perspective changed.

His parents were sympathetic to the civil rights movement in the 1960s. His dad felt so strongly about civil rights, in fact, that at one point he thought about marching with Martin Luther King—though he never actually did. Chris's family, though not liberal in politics or religion, had a sense of the right and wrong of race relations in the United States.

Chris and his family lived in a white suburb on the East Coast, and he went to a predominantly white school. But their house was on the edge of a subdivision that bordered a black section of town known as Jericho. Chris remembers the land in between. Because it was part of the subdivision but hadn't yet been developed, it was still forested, dense with trees; and it made for a great playground. As kids in grade school, he and his white friends played in the yards of houses still under construction, scrambling around the dirt mounds that the bulldozers had created. At times, their play—which often consisted of friendly fights with water balloons and dirt clods—would carry them into the forested area, where they'd hide behind trees and fight battles.

"It was great fun," Chris said. "We were throwing rocks at each other. Somehow no one lost an eye."

Sometimes, a group of black kids from the Jericho subdivision would drift into the same woods to play, and Chris and his friends would see them. Today, he remembers how that was his first childhood sense of white versus black. He remembers his first encounter and being a little scared. But the black kids just marched right on by. One of the white kids said, "Hi," and one of the black kids replied, "Hey." And that was it.

One time, a black teenager named David showed up at Chris's predominantly white church. He, too, lived in the Jericho subdivision. Chris's mom suggested that Chris befriend David and spend some time getting to know him. And Chris did. For a couple of years, they hung out occasionally. Sometimes, Chris's parents would give David a ride to church. Though they went to different schools, they played ball together in the street and would go down to the corner store on summer days to buy Cracker Jacks. By the end of high school, they parted ways. When Chris went off to college, he and David lost touch with each other.

Though Chris's racial attitudes were shaped positively by his friendship with David, they were turned around later in life. Something happened to Chris after he graduated from college. He entered the computer industry, got married, and had kids. All too soon, he found himself stressed by the need to support his family, never quite able to earn as much as they all seemed to need. When his son and daughter graduated from high school and were looking at colleges, Chris—like many parents today—worried about how he would pay for their education. To make matters worse, he faced some setbacks at work and was forced to relocate to another office.

> Some of his work issues had to do with what he perceived to be preferential treatment given to minorities. . . . He gradually developed attitudes and assumptions.

Some of his work issues had to do with what he perceived to be preferential treatment given to minorities in the company. Chris found other things that bothered him as well—about black people in particular. He gradually developed attitudes and assumptions, and he became negative toward these people. He found himself saying things he had never said before. And when incidents of racial conflict popped up on TV, he barked out statements that were judgmental and even prejudiced.

His daughter called him out on it: "You sound like a racist, Dad. Not pretty."

"Thanks," he replied, "I appreciate the gentle delicacy with which you tell me these things."

Despite his sarcasm, her comment hit home. "I don't need to talk like that," he told me, "and I haven't since. Not like that. But, Benjamin, I really do see things differently from you. And I get angry at what governmental policies are doing to white people like me who are trying to make ends meet."

"Tell me more," I replied.

"Okay," he said, "this is nothing against you. You know I respect you. Big time. But I'm working so hard to earn a living and provide for my family, and it's like the government is working against me—and I'll just say it—by preferential treatment to minorities. My son Kevin's college application was turned down, even though his grades and test scores were plenty high enough to get in. But we know someone who knows someone, and apparently there was a minority admissions quota thing. It just doesn't seem fair.

"And," he went on, "my job promotion was in the bag. It had been promised to me for months. And like, I'm careful about these things, not to count on anything until it happens, but it was represented to me as a sure thing. At the last minute, I was told the promotion was on hold. Then, a few days later, I was told I didn't get it. It went to Lissa. She's black. And no accident it's at a time when the company is talking about diversifying its personnel. That's a big deal in the computer industry these days."

"So you're steamed."

"Yeah, I am. Again, I'm not saying I hate black people. It's not like that."

"But you're angry at us."

"Not you, man. Not you. But yes. Angry. Another thing is, I'm frustrated because of the taxes I pay that go to welfare. I see on the news some story about a black mother of three who is scamming the welfare system, saying she has more kids than she has. So, like, I'm thinking, *Great, my money is going to her deceitfulness and lazy lifestyle.*"

Chris finished talking and looked over at me.

"What?" I said. "You want me to solve affirmative action and fix the welfare system?"

"Would you?" he said.

"I'll get right on that. Though it might take till the end of the week."

"No, really, what do you think?"

"I would say some things you don't want to hear."

"That's okay."

"First, you—we—have to make sure we're talking truth. What are the facts? When I hear you talk, so frustrated about these things, I really am sorry they haven't worked out as you hoped. But at the same time, I wonder if all that you assume is true is really true."

"I know what I know, man."

"Yeah. Maybe Kevin *was* passed over because of some affirmative action policy. I know that happens. But in this case, do you really know that for a fact? Is it possible that some other minority student had better grades?"

"Not likely."

"Why? Because that student might have been black? Because it's not likely that a black student could have better grades?"

We tend to take things and automatically blame them on race . . . when sometimes the facts actually say something different.

"I didn't say that."

"But you were thinking it . . ."

"Maybe."

"Not pretty."

"Ouch. Not fair."

"And about the promotion—well, maybe it's true that you didn't get the promotion because this other person was black. But maybe it was actually because she's a woman. Her being black is not the only part of that equation."

"Still—"

"Yes, you still have every reason to feel slighted, even so. I know. I'm just saying we tend to take things and automatically blame them on race. Blacks *and* whites. When sometimes the facts actually say something different."

"I'm pretty sure of the facts."

"Well, maybe so. But I've come to believe that most of what we think is true in these things actually isn't. For example, you're concerned about a black mother scamming the welfare system. But just by sheer population numbers, there are far more white people on welfare than black people. That's a fact. And I imagine that at least a few of those white people are scamming the system too."

"So, that's my point," Chris said. "That feels unfair to me."

"Sure, and I might come alongside you in feeling that way about the welfare system. I pay taxes too. But my point is that you looked at all these injustices that have been done to you, and you immediately assumed they're about racial preference. From a negative attitude toward African Americans, you used these injustices to confirm your antagonism toward black people. You feel justified, then, in saying judgmental things, making racial comments, and expressing that prejudice."

"But Benjamin, sometimes it *is* about racial preference. And that's an injustice that I feel done to me as a white person."

"I know. But there's a lot of injustice to go around. And a lot of injustice *has* gone around. For hundreds of years."

"Sure," Chris said, "but I didn't, and I don't, and I wouldn't ever condone slavery. You know that. But is it my job now to pay for the injustice of slavery back then?"

"Agreed, it shouldn't have to be like that. But I see it like this—if your family were black, living in the '50s, you'd have no chance in American society. You wouldn't be able to go to better schools; you'd be shut out of higher education; you couldn't get significant, better-paying jobs. Your family would have no chance."

"Yeah, yeah, yeah, I know the routine. But, frankly—again, no offense—but I have to think of my family *now*. Not some black family back then."

I had so much more I wanted to say, but sometimes you need to let the conversation sit for a time. There would be other chances to talk with Chris. Though our conversations might sometimes get heated and raw, that can be a good thing—as long as we're honest with each other and as long as both of us know we respect each other.

Though our conversations might sometimes get heated and raw, that can be a good thing—as long as we're honest with each other and respect each other.

I know that Chris's frustration is real and runs deep, and I know it's shared by many other white people in our nation. I know he doesn't want to be a racist, yet much of his anger has been aimed at black people. I think sometimes things happen in the news, and it becomes easy for him to jump to his position and feel confirmed in his attitudes. He's careful about where and how he expresses that, knowing that it's not politically correct; but he finds ample opportunity to vent his prejudice when he's with a group of his friends, or in the privacy of his home. As his daughter observed, Chris is a living-room racist.

Black people do the same. We, too, can be living-room racists. We, too, sit in our homes, in front of the TV, spouting our frustration. We, too, harbor attitudes about white people, and we jump to those racial conclusions when something happens.

We also dismiss the facts too easily. And despite our deepest desire to eliminate racial injustice, we make just about everything that happens a racial issue. Often it is, but sometimes it's simply a tragic event. Still, we jump to our assumptions.

Black people and white people see the world through completely different lenses. The racial divide is about the reality each side sees. Each side believes its view is the true reality, and we can't understand why the other side doesn't see the same thing and understand our reality.

Chris later said that we'd talked so much about his side of things but that he wanted to hear mine. I wrote down a few thoughts and sent them to him:

> I take "our" side because I remember someone threatening to call my sister an "N-word you won't like" back when we were in grade school.

> I take "our" side because of the stares, shadowing, and hollow may-I-help-yous that my wife receives when she shops at a high-end store in an area she's apparently not supposed to be in.

> I take "our" side because whenever I watch news coverage of black people breaking the law, they are called "fatherless thugs," but when a white boy kills nine people at a Bible study, he is said to have "mental problems."

> I confess I have a natural tendency to give people who look like me the benefit of the doubt, especially when it comes to deadly encounters with law enforcement. I just do.

> And I yell at the TV too.

In my e-mail, I added: "While I may be right at times, and history may support my assumptions, am I any better than the white officer who assumes that the black man driving the Range Rover is a drug dealer? In light of our black history, it's so much easier to prejudge. It's actually more comfortable and easier than approaching each case and each person as an individual."

My conversations with Chris may never change him—or me. But I think it's good to continue the dialogue. It may not change our minds, but it might change our views ever so slightly.

If, God forbid, there's another Ferguson, maybe Chris will see on his TV, in place of the next Michael Brown, the image of his friend Benjamin. And maybe I'll see, just for a moment, the image of my friend Chris in the face of the next Darren Wilson.

. . .

We want to point our fingers outward, but the problem of race starts within.

At an early age, we seem to accept people who are different from us. But judgments soon form. We grow up learning certain subtle attitudes toward other races from our families, our schools, and our neighborhoods.

We develop harsher racial ideas from the people we hang out with. We want to fit in.

We experience something harsh or hurtful, and we point to the perpetrators—they're white. Or they're black. We generalize about an entire race.

We form an assumption. We form additional assumptions. We form a quiet prejudice.

> Deep in their hearts, millions of ordinary people like you and me . . . hold certain opinions, assumptions, and prejudices toward the other race.

Deep in their hearts, millions of ordinary people like you and me—seemingly good people who consider themselves fair and unbiased, who have black and white friends—hold certain opinions, assumptions, and prejudices toward the other race.

That's the problem.

Racial solutions won't be found in political reactions to Ferguson or Charleston. They won't be found in laws that clamp down on supremacy groups, or in finding scapegoats in the FBI for lax gun checks. They won't be found in massive government programs that try to force-fix the problems of human behavior.

Racial solutions will never be found in pointing fingers at a culture of white supremacy, the KKK, or hate groups.

And racial solutions will never be found in pointing the finger at Dylann Roof or others of his ilk, suggesting that he epitomizes the problem of race.

The solution to the problem of race in America will be found only by ordinary people, "good" people, looking inside themselves, being honest about the assumptions and biases that have formed, and beginning to change what's in their hearts.

I have to look inside my own heart and see what lurks there, what assumptions about white people I've formed, and what prejudices I still harbor.

I confess I have prejudices and I make assumptions about white people as a whole, even though some of those assumptions have been proven wrong through individual relationships. I confess that I generalize such prejudices across the entire race.

I confess I've harbored thoughts against white people that, while perhaps not harshly racist, have been judgmental and hurtful.

I confess I've said things in private that have been prejudiced and judgmental about white people I have seen, heard, or read about.

I confess . . .

. . .

Immediately after the Charleston tragedy, Mike Johnston, a Colorado state senator from Denver, did an unusual thing. In the middle of the night, he drove to Shorter AME Church in downtown Denver and posted a letter on the church's front door. The letter read, in part:

> My heart breaks for those children of God that we lost in your sister church in South Carolina tonight. On a night when old, devastating patterns of racial injustice return like childhood nightmares, it seemed the best thing to do was to get out of my bed and drive over here to make sure this note was the first thing you saw when you walked in the church tomorrow. This white man is driving over to this AME church to tell you how deeply grateful I am that the leaders of your church have helped build this city, and how honored I am that the ancestors of this church have helped build this great country.[3]

Johnston later invited others to "make a small but powerful statement . . . by stopping by any AME church . . . and perform a quiet act of service and leave a humble note of thanks."[4]

Two days after the shooting, at a court hearing for Dylann Roof, the families of the victims had a chance to confront him. One by one, they stood up, clearly battling deep emotion, spoke to Roof—and *forgave* him.

Alana Simmons, who had lost her grandfather in the tragedy, said: "Although my grandfather and the other victims died at the hands of hate, this is proof—everyone's plea for your soul is proof that they lived in love and their legacies will live in love, so hate won't win."[5]

Felicia Sanders was one of the survivors; she made it through by pretending to be dead. But her son, Tywanza, was one of the victims that night. In court, Felicia said to Dylann Roof: "We welcomed you Wednesday night in our Bible study with open arms. You have killed some of the most beautifulest people that I know. Every fiber in my body hurts . . . and I'll never be the same. . . . Tywanza was my hero. But as we said in Bible study, we enjoyed you but may God have mercy on you."[6]

Among the many memorials and observances for the victims, one thing became clear: There is a unique power within the human heart to overcome hate and racism.

■   ■   ■

Not long ago, I reconnected with Bert, my childhood friend.

Bert is now a relief captain for a tugboat towing firm in northern Virginia. He told me that his dad is a Virginia state pilot, one who boards ships when they come near land to help guide them into port.

Bert and I reminisced about our boyhood days and our fond memories of the creek. We laughed about the venison sloppy joes, our adventures along the river, and crabbing under the bridge. He teased me about not knowing what a minnow was, and I made a point in return about all the fishing he'd done while rarely ever catching a fish.

It felt good to talk with him again, to go back in our minds to those lazy summer days sitting on the dock.

I don't think he and I said anything about race. It never mattered.

And that's kind of the point.

Among the many memorials and observances for the victims, one thing became clear: There is a unique power within the human heart to overcome hate and racism.

EMBARRASSED

I'M EMBARRASSED
because the looting, violent protests, and lawbreaking
only confirm—and in the minds of many, validate—
the stereotypes and thus the inferior treatment.

THE MOVIE *SELMA* depicts the events of a period in our history when black people fought the system. And won.

It was 1965—a long time ago, and yet not such a long time. It's hard for me to believe that in the same decade when men walked on the moon, black people still did not have the vote. Oh, we had the *right* to vote on paper, just not in practice. It's hard for me to believe that many states and counties intentionally created an abusive and arbitrary voting-registration process that kept black people unregistered—and afraid, for reasons of physical safety, of even trying to register. It's hard for me to believe that in 1965, three years *after* the Rolling Stones formed as a rock band, segregation was still an approved social and legal policy practiced widely in the United States.

It's hard for me to believe that, one hundred years after the end of the Civil War and the abolition of slavery, America was still stuck in a maze of Jim Crow laws; still enforcing the "separate but equal" doctrine; still keeping Negroes apart while winking at the Constitution's assertion of equality; and still protecting and condoning police harassment and brutal treatment of blacks for no good reason other than that a black person looked them in the eye or didn't, moved or didn't, said something or didn't.

It's hard for me to believe that in 1965 black people were still denied the right to assemble—that most basic of Constitutional rights—and were prevented from conducting a march and organizing a peaceful protest. This is what black people had to fight against back then. They had to *fight* for the right to protest peacefully.

This is the world of *Selma*.

It was in that world that four young Negro girls were play-ing on the stairway of an old Birmingham church when fifteen sticks of dynamite exploded. It was later found to be the work of the Ku Klux Klan, a white supremacy group that somehow, in its cloaked and hooded courage, believed there was a noble cause to be won by bombing a church and killing four little girls.

> It's hard for me to believe that in 1965 black people were denied the right to assemble . . . and were prevented from conducting a march and organizing a peaceful protest.

But that was *then*. Right?

Sadly, that was then and this is now: Fifty years later and 450 miles east of that Birmingham church building, a young white man entered a church in Charleston and shot to death nine black people in the name of white supremacy.

Selma captures a critical moment in the story of blacks and whites in America: how black people rose up in a nonviolent way and changed the political equation, how the political machine of the old South began to topple, and how white people from across the country came alongside black people in the march for change.

Specifically, the film depicts one of the many civil rights marches of the 1950s and '60s—the march from Selma to Montgomery, organized by Martin Luther King Jr. to address the white establishment's persistent sabotage of black voter registration.

The planned march began tragically. On Sunday, March 7, 1965, about six hundred African Americans set out from Selma to the state capital of Montgomery to protest voter registration practices. But they never even got out of town. On the far side of the Edmund Pettus Bridge, just south of downtown Selma, some 150 Alabama state troopers and other law enforcement officers, led by a police car bearing a Confederate flag on the front license plate panel, formed a line to intercept the march and literally beat it back.[1] The troopers bludgeoned the marchers with billy clubs, leaving men and women writhing on the roadway. When the marchers knelt in a prayerful posture, the troopers used tear gas to disperse them.[2] The day became known as Bloody Sunday.

Against all odds, two days later they tried again. *Selma* shows the drama of that moment, with the marchers—many of whom were still bandaged from wounds suffered on the previous march—once again crossing the Edmund Pettus Bridge and once again facing a line of Alabama state troopers. This time, the troopers opened their ranks, seeming to invite the marchers through. But Martin Luther King, sensing a ploy and a trap, knelt on the bridge to pray instead. One by one, the other marchers knelt and prayed as well. Soon, Dr. King turned the march around for fear of violence, and the protesters returned home.

The film acknowledges that Dr. King was criticized for turning back from that second attempt and that some of his advisers felt that a more aggressive, violent approach was needed.

I think perhaps this tension has always been a part of the black-white story. In the 1960s, it was the difference between Dr. King, the Nobel Peace Prize winner, and Malcolm X, whose doctrine of black supremacy led to violent action and rioting. It is still true today among many who advocate confrontation and violence as the only effective means for change. Some argue that throughout history white supremacy has been the prevailing evil that has plagued civilization.

I think there's another story to tell.

What changed the equation in March 1965 was, quite simply,

television. When the events of Bloody Sunday were captured on film and the police brutality was broadcast across the country, many Americans—white Americans—were horrified. What they saw was an embarrassment of violence perpetrated by white cops and a racist white state government.

When the events of Bloody Sunday were broadcast across the country, many Americans— white Americans— were horrified.

Not quite two weeks later, the marchers tried again. This time, Alabama governor George Wallace tried to prevent the demonstration from happening, but the marchers won in district court. President Lyndon Johnson ordered US Army and National Guard forces to protect the marchers along the way.

The marchers left Selma on March 21, some two thousand strong. Along the way, they were joined by others—and not just by black brothers and sisters but by white supporters as well—people from all over the country. By the time they reached Montgomery and Dr. King walked up the steps to the state capitol, the crowd had swelled to fifty thousand people, both black and white, joined together in extraordinary unity.[3]

Dr. King declared that "no tide of racism can stop us."[4] He recited some of the lyrics to "The Battle Hymn of the Republic": "Mine eyes have seen the glory of the coming of the Lord."

The Selma to Montgomery march, a determined but peaceful protest, forced the hand of politicians who until then had resisted change. About four months later, Congress passed the Voting Rights Act of 1965, which established oversight, reforms, and needed changes to voter registration practices across the country.

Some might say that the film *Selma* is the story of Martin Luther King Jr. I disagree. Though *Selma* features him as a main character and there is much he did that effectively directed the Selma march, the real hero of the story, as I see it, was the irrepressible dignity of African Americans in that time and place.

I think about what they experienced and endured: the denial of legal rights; the consistent maltreatment; and being looked upon as inferior, subhuman, and even as animals. To think that they had to overcome restrictions against the fundamental rights of assembly and protest. To think that they had to endure physical attacks, abuse, and injury—not only from white-supremacist and racist organizations but also at the hands of law enforcement, whose mandate has always been to protect and serve.

How would I have responded if I had been alive then?

The injustice is so overwhelming and tragic that my instinct would be to lash out, to respond in kind, to fight violence with violence. I get it, believe me. You could justify protest and protection, objecting to the heinous wrongs while defending your friends and family, not to mention yourself.

And yet the marchers in Selma didn't do that.

They fought violence with nonviolence. They fought hate speech with prayer. They fought indignity by rising up in all the glory of their God-given humanity.

> They fought violence with nonviolence. They fought hate speech with prayer. They fought indignity by rising up in all the glory of their God-given humanity.

. . .

I compare the images from Selma to the images from Ferguson.

In Selma, the faces that stick with me are not those of Martin Luther King or Andrew Young or any of the other black leaders involved in the march. I see only the faces of the women who marched that day. In my mind's eye, I see their faces, reflecting at once the emotions of fear and faith, hurt and hope; their eyes, focused on changing the reality of life, perhaps not for themselves but for their children; their lips, praying for deliverance, not so much from the white state troopers as from a life and future of indignity. I see their conviction rising with every step they take, as they draw closer to the steps of the capitol building in Montgomery as if it were the Promised Land: closer to the glory of a new day and closer to the glory of God himself. You cannot separate the black struggle from faith in God.

And now I have the searing images of Ferguson imprinted on my mind as well.

I see black people burning cars or raiding convenience stores—and as a black man, I'm embarrassed. I'm not dismissing the pain of perceived injustice, and I defend the right to protest; but the violence of that night in Ferguson was not about protesting injustice. It was about committing crime. It was about self. It was about using a tragedy to grab something unearned—whether an LCD TV or the attention of a TV news reporter. Destroying or stealing someone else's property, robbing someone who had nothing to do with the inciting transgression, is not only criminal but also makes a huge visual statement to the world about the events of that night. It confirms the worst stereotypes. And it undoes the purpose, spirit, and progress that those peaceful marchers fought for fifty years ago in Selma.

> Destroying or stealing someone else's property . . . undoes the purpose, spirit, and progress that those peaceful marchers fought for fifty years ago in Selma.

It becomes an embarrassment of violence.

■   ■   ■

One thing about Selma pops out. Television was a significant factor in communicating throughout the country the events of those days. Fifty thousand people showed up in Montgomery largely because of the television coverage of the police brutality two weeks earlier. In the early 1960s, the power of TV had already become a new reality in politics, playing an important role in the 1960 presidential campaign between Nixon and Kennedy. In 1965, it became a factor in the struggle for civil rights.

We look at television back then as a positive force for change. Apparently, it helped fuel the reforms that came from Selma. But I think it's worth imagining a different course of action—one in which the marchers responded instead with violence and chaos. What would have happened then?

In fact, we know what would have happened—because it *did* happen. Only five months after Selma, the Watts riots in Los Angeles erupted, prompted by a traffic stop of a black man who resisted arrest and by a crowd that formed, protesting the arrest.

The Watts section of LA was predominantly black, overcrowded, and plagued by a high unemployment rate. Of the 205 cops assigned to Watts, 200 were white.[5] During the long hot summer of 1965, Watts exploded, literally, in flames.

The images were captured on television—a still relatively new medium that was growing in influence. Some whites watched the broadcasts and thought blacks were crazy to burn down their own neighborhoods. More rioting in Newark and Detroit in 1967, again shown on TV, continued to galvanize the black-white divide. Black people were angry, and rightfully so, but they were perceived as destructive and dangerous by white people.

The immediacy of television, which had been the downfall of Richard Nixon during the 1960 presidential debates with Kennedy, now gave white America reason to put Nixon, the law-and-order candidate, in the White House. Nicolaus Mills observes, "For [Martin Luther] King and the president [Lyndon Johnson], who had helped make 1965 such a triumphal year in civil rights, the Watts riots came at the worst possible time. The riots undercut the political momentum created by Selma and set in motion a white backlash that would last for years and, in 1968, help propel Richard Nixon to the presidency."[6]

Today, it's much different. And yet not so different.

The Watts riots undercut the political momentum created by Selma and set in motion a white backlash that would last for years.

Today, the term *media* comprises many sources, as we all know—TV news cameras; cell phone videos that anyone and everyone can capture at any time; social media filled with uncensored and unconsidered comments; network, cable, satellite, and online programs that focus on shouting-match debates; and reporting that transmits news in pieces, without context, often jumping to false conclusions.

One thing that many of us, black and white, can agree on is that the media presence in Ferguson fueled the fires.

Kathleen Parker of the *Washington Post* writes: "To the extent that people clown, plunder or pillage for attention, media presence does make a difference. Cameras not only capture the action but in some cases may well prompt the action. . . . A bad day in America is a good day in the newsroom."[7] The presence of cameras changes the scene. And TV news applauds.

Social media—tools for people to transmit messages instantly to each other in real time via Facebook, Twitter, Reddit, Instagram, etc.—also affect the scene. Some of this is positive, as people at ground zero transmit information we might not have had otherwise. But I would argue that some social media platforms can also falsely report impressions as facts, opinion as truth, and emotions as cause. Social media apps often dribble out information that is incomplete and lacks context, leading to interpretations that are flat-out wrong. Who of us hasn't had to untangle hurt feelings and misperceptions with family members because of things carelessly and casually posted on Facebook?

Don't get me wrong: Of all people, I am one who understands the power of thoughtful, reasoned articles posted on social media. But I have to think that there are dangers when our source of news in the heat of the moment are the tweets of people, on any side, who are emotionally "reporting" what they think (and want to believe) is true.

Anyone who follows a major news story knows that you can talk to ten people over the course of the event and hear ten different accounts of what went down. And TV news people are notorious for broadcasting inferences and theories in the absence of facts. I mean, they have to fill the time, right? Unfortunately, according to psychologists, it's harder to correct an inference or hypothesis than it is to correct a false statement. Studies show that test groups who are fed statements that suggest "this or that might have happened" find it difficult later to let go of those hypothetical scenarios, even when the facts prove something very different.[8] Sadly, so much of what constitutes TV news these days is speculative reporting. Eric Horowitz writes, "The studies paint a damning picture of a behavior at the core of how media organizations deliver content."[9] As the subhead to the Horowitz article says, "It may seem reasonable for on-air talent to fill airtime with speculation and predictions, but it's more difficult for us to correct that sort of misinformation later on."[10]

> When TV news is chock-full of newscasters forming theories and assumptions, most which later prove to be untrue, they contribute to the problem.

When TV news is chock-full of newscasters forming theories and assumptions, most of which later prove to be untrue, they contribute to the problem and become part of the story. Research has also shown that when these speculative and theoretical statements confirm a person's deeply held beliefs, they are even harder to correct. Of course, this principle applies on both sides of the racial divide. Whether we are prone to believe that an injustice was done to Michael Brown or to Darren Wilson, countless newscasters and commentators made the problem worse among viewers by speculating about what *might* have happened when the facts were unclear.

Of course, we feel better when we have photos to look at or video to watch. When we can watch something, we think we're getting the truth. We tend to view visual evidence as absolute. During events such as the ones swirling around Ferguson, thousands of images are posted online in the heat of the moment, and we think we have the story. But we should know better. Anyone who watches instant replay on an NFL broadcast knows how different something looks from an alternate angle. We see the video of a wide receiver catching the ball and stepping out of bounds. But wait! Did he have two feet down? Was he bobbling the ball or did he have control before he stepped out? And after a dozen replays, the debate still rages in your living room with your buddies.

So let me ask you: Why do traditional news outlets report what people say on Twitter? Don't they know that such tweets are likely in error? Don't they know that people posting on social media have a viewpoint, a bias, or maybe an ax to grind? Is there no effort made anymore to get the facts right? Is there no desire for objective reporting?

The Ferguson grand jury determined that initial eyewitness reports—on both sides—were unreliable.[11] People later changed their stories or recanted their testimony under oath. Newscasters who reported on the basis of those eyewitness reports, postings, and tweets simply got it wrong. There was much speculation about whether Michael Brown had been shot in the back. Autopsy evidence said no. The grand jury decided not to indict.

There were some notable anomalies in the grand jury proceedings. Though not supposed to be a court trial, the Ferguson grand jury was nonetheless presented with *all* the evidence, as if it were a court trial. The defendant, Darren Wilson, testified, which is highly unusual for a grand jury procedure.[12] Perhaps the conflicting reports and false testimony convinced the jurors not to indict. Or maybe the presentation of all the extraneous information simply served to confuse the issue.[13]

And yet some facts remained and were verified: Darren Wilson fired his weapon twelve times. Michael Brown was hit at least six times.[14] He was thirty feet away from Darren Wilson when the final shots were fired. And he was unarmed.

I don't know why the jurors came to the conclusion they did. Maybe it was well considered. Some feel that the grand jury "got it right." I just wonder whether all the mainstream-media buzz and social-media chatter clouded the truth on both sides, making it murky enough that the real truth was impossible to decipher. Social media and TV news can get a lot of things wrong. And they often do.

But nothing riles me more about the media circus than all the talking heads propped up on what are said to be TV news shows—self-important commentators intentionally paired off in heated, loud, fierce debate. I don't care whose side you're on—those canned shouting matches do not shed light on anything. They are not *news*. And they only deepen people's entrenchment in the positions they already have. These contrived TV debates are far more about winning an argument than about getting at the truth.

> Nothing riles me more about the media circus than all the talking heads . . . paired off in heated, loud, fierce debate.

Here's what's really bad about those shows: They reduce every issue or event to a debate. And this approach spills out of the TV studios and into our lives. We become all about "taking a side" and arguing it fiercely. We then look for facts to fit our assumptions. And we learn to distrust everything that doesn't fit our version of reality.

And all of this simply divides us.

Truth is often more complex than we want it to be. And it's easier to paint ourselves as white or black, either/or, rather than both/and. Could it be that Michael Brown *both* did something wrong *and* did not deserve to be shot six times? Could it be that Darren Wilson *both* was just doing his job *and* responded inappropriately to a perceived threat?

It's hard to convince black people that Michael Brown, and others like him, didn't suffer a grave wrong. Black people who have repeatedly experienced police bias and profiling, and who have the historical memory of being attacked by state troopers on that Selma road fifty years ago, just aren't buying the official line. It's hard to convince us that sometimes these things "just happen" or that it's simply a tragic mistake. Too many things "just happen" to black people.

But likewise, I know it's hard to convince many white people that a big, powerful young man like Michael Brown was innocent, didn't disobey Wilson's orders, and didn't threaten a cop who was actually doing the right thing. I know what my friend Chris would say: "You're just choosing to see this through your set of glasses. Brown was a thief. He ran. He was guilty."

I would jab back: "He shouldn't be *shot* for stealing cigars."

Chris would shrug. "Just sayin', if you're innocent, you don't need to run."

"That's *your* set of glasses. If you're black, you know you don't stand much of a chance in the hands of a cop."

And before you know it, I'm just another one of those talking heads shouting in angry debate.

That's the crux of the problem with the racial divide. It's a *divide.* We can't help but slide to one side of the ring or the other and get ready to fight.

And the media pundits push us toward our respective corners.

. . .

I wonder why we can't learn from Ferguson.

I wonder why the next time—and there will be a next time—we can't vow to refrain from quick judgments in the first hours, and even days, of a tragedy. I wonder why we can't keep from leaping to the conclusion that our side was wronged.

I wonder why we can't be more cautious about social media in those early hours and wisely decide that most early commentary in a situation will be flawed.

I wonder why we can't turn off the TV when the speculators and the sparring matches come on; and why we can't keep from going to our respective corners; and why we can't have the courage to stay away from groupthink.

> I wonder why we can't learn from Ferguson. . . . I wonder why we can't keep from leaping to the conclusion that our side was wronged.

I wonder why, next time, we can't choose the dignity of peace over the embarrassment of violence.

I wonder why we can't refuse to let the media sway us and tell us how to think, and why we have to turn every incident into commentary on politics and race.

I wonder why we can't, for even just a few moments, consider a life that was lost and another that was shattered; and why in these times of great tragedy we can't understand that we share something deep and beautiful, that we all share the same heritage—we share a common humanity. We are all created by the same God.

. . .

I believe that the great struggle in the racial divide is not about finding agreement on all issues. That will never happen—though I confess that part of my hope in writing this is that I'll be able to articulate thoughts and ideas and opinions that will bring us together in some significant way. But I'm realistic, too. I know that by and large we will stay segregated in our corners and groups and will continue to sit in the comfortable hot tub of our entrenched opinions. I hope for more, but I understand how difficult it is to change.

No, the great struggle for blacks and whites is not in finding political or social agreement. It won't be found in legislation, government programs, or election results.

The great struggle for blacks and whites is to accept each other on the basis of our common humanity, a humanity that comes, as I believe, from God.

Genetic research shows that the races are really not as different as we think. In fact, we're hardly different at all. Speaker and author Ken Ham reports on the research regarding the biology of racial differences:

> The truth . . . is that these so-called "racial characteristics"
> are only minor variations among people groups. If one
> were to take any two people anywhere in the world,
> scientists have found that the basic genetic differences
> between these two people would typically be around
> 0.2 percent—even if they came from the same people
> group. But these so-called "racial" characteristics that
> people think are major differences (skin color, eye shape,
> etc.) "account for only 0.012 percent of human biological
> variation."[15]

Anthropologist Ashley Montagu's classic book *Man's Most Dangerous Myth: The Fallacy of Race* says, "The idea of 'race' represents one of the most dangerous myths of our time, and one of the most tragic."[16] Francis Collins—head of the Human Genome Project for a decade and a half, an outspoken Christian, and bestselling author of *The Language of God*—has said that all human DNA is "99.9 percent identical."[17] While that remaining 0.1 percent is being deeply researched, it too reveals that such differences are not racial in origin. Geneticist Duana Fullwiley says, "There is no genetic basis for race."[18]

This is not to say that there are no biological differences at all, just that genetics point to a minuscule percentage of difference between racial groups. The greater differences we see and think are racial have much more to do with geography and culture. To scientists, the racial classification of Caucasian, for example, has little biological significance. It matters more that your DNA shows an ancestry in northern Europe or Asia or Africa. Your physical traits, and mine, have more to do with our ancestors adapting to the geography and cultures of a place than with the genetics of a race. According to these scientists, as an African American I am far more genetically similar to many of my Caucasian friends than they are to certain other Caucasians. Race is literally only skin deep.

We are commonly human.

Of course, race *does* exist—but science proclaims it to be far more of a social understanding than a scientific one. We classify each other according to race, and it serves a purpose—to name and identify social and cultural distinctions. And please hear me—we should preserve and celebrate our cultural differences, embrace the uniqueness of our histories, and pursue the

> **Genetics point to a minuscule percentage of difference between racial groups. . . . Race is literally only skin deep.**

distinctiveness of our arts and enterprises. We are beautifully different. But we are commonly human.

Throughout history, many have bought into the social construct of race, taught generations of people that it is biologically and genetically rooted, and used this false genetic understanding of race as a weapon to create notions of superiority and to instill feelings of inferiority.

In other words, we ourselves are the cause of the racial divide. By our history, by our culture, and most of all by the politics of race.

How much has the traditional view of racial genetics determined the course of human history? How much did it fuel the underlying justification for black slavery from its origins in the 1600s? To what extent did these assumptions permit slavery to be institutionalized? How much was this understanding of race assumed to be a biblical and Christian defense of black slavery?

We know all too well how the myth of racial genetics was used as a rationale for the philosophy of Nazism, the unthinkable effort to create a pure Aryan race, and the systematic attempt to exterminate the Jews.

Legacies of racial inequality and group supremacy can be found in many countries, regions, and cultures throughout history. It's useful for those in the ruling classes—whether in China, Brazil, the Middle East, Europe, the United States, or even Africa—to bludgeon others for being *born different*. If you are born different, you are born into a status you can't change. So the myth is perpetuated. And by exploiting that myth, those in power can maintain their power and keep entire groups of people subjugated.

Wielding that myth and preaching the inferiority of blacks, the white political establishment in 1965 Alabama, epitomized by governor George Wallace, tried to keep black Americans "in their place." Wallace's government did it by intimidation, manipulation of the voting-registration process, brutal physical violence, and the power of law enforcement. But as the establishment tried to institutionalize the myth of white superiority, it demonstrated only one thing to the rest of the nation—the embarrassment of violence.

The white supremacists could not stop the movement of African Americans across Alabama. They could not repress the spirit of marchers, a spirit that rippled across the nation to other blacks as well as whites. They could not stop a race from expressing their inherent, God-given human dignity.

Through peaceful protest, those who marched on the road from Selma to Montgomery demonstrated how it should be done.

As the establishment tried to institutionalize the myth of white superiority, it demonstrated only one thing to the rest of the nation—the embarrassment of violence.

. . .

One thing I loved about the film *Selma* was seeing in that final march all the white Northerners who came to march alongside their Southern black brothers and sisters. Men and women of all ages; pastors, priests, nuns, and church people; people from east and west—so many came to support the cause of African Americans in the Deep South.

I know there are some who are cynical about Northern white involvement in the civil rights marches in the South. Some people suggest that the whites came only when it became "the thing to do." Where were they weeks, months, or years earlier? Or for that matter, many decades earlier?

Well, I'm not one of those cynics. I think something is tremendously *right* when blacks and whites march together, joining hands to overthrow an abusive and offensive political system. If even for a brief moment in time, it underscores and affirms common humanity.

I think something is tremendously *right* when blacks and whites march together, joining hands to overthrow an abusive and offensive political system.

We all know that only three years after the Selma march, Martin Luther King Jr. was shot and killed in Memphis. What many don't know is that during the last year of his life he organized something called the Poor People's Campaign, an effort to pressure the president and Congress, through a peaceful march on Washington, DC, to "pass substantial anti-poverty legislation" and "help the poor get jobs, health care and decent homes."[19] The movement was controversial for a number of reasons, perhaps most of all because it wasn't just for black people.

It was for poor white people, too.

FRUSTRATED

I'M FRUSTRATED
because pop culture, music, and movies glorify
these types of police-citizen altercations . . .

In my teens, I developed a love affair with hip-hop.

For me, it started when Snoop Dogg released his debut album, *Doggystyle*. I was thirteen. All my friends in the neighborhood were into the latest artists and albums. Though we might sometimes listen to rock or pop, hip-hop was our music. In the early '90s hip-hop was becoming more mainstream, finding new fans beyond its early roots. My friends and I were some of those new young fans.

At the time, my family was once again living in Norfolk, where I was born. We had moved away for a few years so that Daddy could go to seminary in Columbia, South Carolina. Having felt the call to pastor a church, he believed he needed seminary training to be truly qualified.

In the early '70s, when he was a teenager, the story goes that he looked up at the stars one night and called out to God: "If you reveal yourself to me, I will follow you." A few days later, he happened to be watching TV and saw Billy Graham preaching at one of his famous crusades. In those moments, my dad got saved. After that, he was on fire for God, preaching wherever they would let him. He saw everything in life as a potential sermon illustration. In fact, it became a running joke among us kids to find the most common, ordinary thing and say, "Now there's a *sermon illustration* in that."

After a couple of years in South Carolina, we moved back to Norfolk. I was around ten when we moved, and it wasn't long before I discovered a new music and a new rhythm to live by.

Hip-hop has its roots in '70s soul and funk styles and is a uniquely African American form, with its rhythmic chanting, synthesized instruments, and urban poetry. Originating in New York City, it emerged as not only an urban music but also an expression of urban black culture. I know that a lot of people don't understand hip-hop, but for my friends and me, it spoke our language. When I encountered it in the early '90s, to my ears it was a complex, intense, and extraordinary sound. And somehow it put words to my life.

I know that a lot of people don't understand hip-hop, but for my friends and me, it spoke our language. . . . And somehow it put words to my life.

In 1993, there was a battle of sorts between East Coast and West Coast rap. East Coast artists Notorious B.I.G., Nas, and A Tribe Called Quest developed a hip-hop sound that was more jazz-derivative; West Coast rappers Dr. Dre, Tupac, and Ice Cube had more of a new-funk sound, which became known as G-funk.

For most of us fans, the style didn't matter—the rap-music scene was exploding. And though we lived in southeast Virginia, we all wanted to be a part of what was happening in New York and LA.

Including Stanley and me.

Stanley was black like me, though lighter skinned: one of a group of guys with whom I played football in the street. The streets in our neighborhood of Campostella Heights were two-lane but narrow, with short curbs and a strip of grass along either side. We played football out in the middle of the road, with tackling permitted on the grassy patch along the side. People think about that and consider it dangerous, but it wasn't so much. No one got hurt—well, not too often. Scraped knees and arms were all in a day's fun. We gave our teams names—the Playmakers or the All-Stars—and we'd play late into the evening sometimes, under the streetlights.

My friend Stanley was a couple years older than I was and already in high school. He was quite the dresser and somehow had all the cool clothes back then—Karl Kani jeans and high-top FILAs with the strap. As if that wasn't cool enough, Stanley was also a drummer.

Drums were his thing, and he could kick beats all day. You'd walk by his house and hear him on his drum set, practicing a riff over and over and over. I think even then, as a teenager, I felt sorry for his mom and dad, listening to the snare and bass drums all day long. But Stanley was a good player, and he was very much into music—all kinds, from gospel to pop to hip-hop. He had more hip-hop tapes and albums than I had ever seen.

I remember it like it was yesterday: Stanley handing me the *Doggystyle* tape and telling me to go home and check it out. Snoop Dogg was a protégé of Dr. Dre and had collaborated with Dre on the album *The Chronic*, which had quickly become a classic. Wanting to be down with it, I took the tape, not realizing that the album included one of the hottest (and roughest) songs of the day, "Gin and Juice." I brought the tape home, intending to pop it into my old black Sony tape player sometime when my parents and siblings weren't around to overhear.

I took the tape, not realizing that the album included one of the hottest (and roughest) songs of the day.

I didn't have time for it that evening, and I rose early the next morning to get ready for school. To offset the cost of school in those days, my mother drove the school bus, so my sister and I were always the first to leave and the last to get home every day. Unfortunately, I shared a bedroom with my five-year-old brother, Matthew. He had a habit of meddling in my stuff, a habit that often led to a brotherly fight when I returned home from school on weekday afternoons. On this particular day, Matthew decided that instead of pouring out my cologne or tearing up my Lego tower, it would be great fun to pop Stanley's Snoop Dogg tape into the cassette recorder and play "Gin and Juice" at full volume.

All I know is that when I got home, my father was waiting for me. He called me upstairs immediately, tape in hand, and I knew he had heard some of the music. With anger on his face, sucking his teeth in deep disappointment, he warned me to never bring filth like that into his house again. It was a moment I'll remember for the rest of my life. Tears streamed down my cheeks as I faced him. It wasn't that I had made him angry; it was that I had disappointed him so badly.

If I hadn't been so ashamed, I might have known that this would become another sermon illustration for Daddy. But in the moment, I didn't care—I had only one thought. I remember taking the tape from my dad's hand, running out the front door, and sprinting the two blocks to Stanley's house. Then I threw the tape onto his front porch with a yell of disgust.

. . .

It's too simplistic to condemn an entire genre of music for one song on one tape. And frankly, I didn't. Because of that incident, my love affair with the music of Snoop Dogg was over, but I admit that I continued to enjoy hip-hop for years to come.

Yes, my love for hip-hop continued to grow. Staten Island's Wu-Tang Clan became my favorite during my teenage years. They were quintessential East Coast style, one of the greatest hip-hop groups of all time, classic. They took their name from the 1983 martial arts movie *Shaolin and Wu Tang*, and in their debut album they sampled the movie's soundtrack, mixing soul samples; piano keys; hard beats; and rough, gritty vocals that had all of us, black and white, imitating the Wu.

During college, the music of Jay-Z and the Southern rap sound of Outkast accompanied me through many pregame bus rides to stadiums in Tuscaloosa, Baton Rouge, Columbia, and Athens. Hip-hop kept me awake and energized as I burned the midnight oil studying for exams. Lil Jon and his crunk music were a favorite for postgame celebrations downtown.

So that's my confession. I still like—and still listen to—hip-hop.

Music of all kinds allows us to express a range of human emotions: sadness and anger, joy and elation. It's a language voicing the highest and lowest points of life, an art that comes from the heart and soul. It's a way to broadcast political, social, and relational experiences. All genres of music—pop, rock, blues, jazz, and hip-hop—are means by which we sometimes cry, laugh, or scream at the world.

Hip-hop kept me awake and energized as I burned the midnight oil studying for exams. . . . So that's my confession. I still like—and still listen to—hip-hop.

This is a conversation we all can have about our favorite music, movies, television, and video games—the stuff that fills our hearts and minds and lives. As entertainment, it's sometimes just fun, but often it's more: the rhythms and images and words that touch lives. Our lives.

Of all music genres, hip-hop is probably the form that is most extreme and most raw. It is a music of anger. It is a music of passion. It is a music of protest. And as a vehicle for protest, hip-hop is uniquely African American. Like blues and R & B, much of hip-hop is a storytelling form, echoing an oral tradition that is at the core of black history and drawing the listener into the frustration and protest of the artist.

At its best, hip-hop is the urban poetry of a generation of young black people.

It has been my music. A music that expresses so much of what's inside me. A music I confess I sometimes love.

But it's a love-hate relationship.

In recent years, my devotion to hip-hop has waned. As I've gotten older, some of hip-hop's desperation has begun to seem overacted. Maybe it's like grunge today for white people who grew up listening to Nirvana. Sure, when certain groups and songs play, I smile, remembering the anthem of the time and how it became the background soundtrack for my life at a particular time and place. But more often than not, some hip-hop just seems relentlessly tiring. Perhaps now I've begun to walk away from hip-hop because I have a family. I find it hard these days to listen to some of the lyrics. Maybe I struggle now with hip-hop because I have a career and a place in life, and with those things comes a sense of responsibility and purpose—experiences that are generally not found in hip-hop.

I struggle now with hip-hop because I have a career and a place in life, and with those things comes a sense of responsibility and purpose.

But primarily, my relationship with hip-hop has waned because of a deeper, clearer look at what I've found to be its true nature.

People decried the influence of rock music when it came on the scene in the '50s and '60s, arguing that the rhythms and beats somehow seeped into our brains and affected our behavior. And there does seem to be a biological connection between music and certain hormones that affect our emotions.[1] The beats move us, release hormones, activate our bodies, and make us feel emotions in a deeper way. Through music, we feel things more vividly. This is true for all music, not just for rock or hip-hop. Clearly, music affects us deeply.

Some research on the relationship between music and stress

hormones suggests that certain kinds of music relieve stress.[2] Research also points to some music that can increase stress. The neuroscience behind this is still in its infancy, and there is much we don't know. But it's not a leap of logic to suggest that music moves us emotionally in deep and significant ways.

More and more, I believe that the music of hip-hop in particular captures our minds and bodies. I'm not saying it *causes* us to act out in negative ways, but I think it can contribute to negative behaviors. I know from personal experience how hip-hop becomes a personal background soundtrack. It makes one feel empowered and invincible. What if that soundtrack is accompanied by messages that express frustration, anger, and hatred? What if those messages become a kind of battle cry that calls people to violence?

I believe hip-hop does that.

My struggle with hip-hop is that I feel the tension between two very important aspects of the genre. On the one hand, I defend its blackness. I defend its expression of the experience of race. I defend it as a poetry of life in black, urban America. But on the other hand, I cannot condone the message it often preaches or the values it underscores.

I know exactly why my father was so incensed that evening when he heard the Snoop Dogg tape playing in my room. I knew then and I know now. It wasn't the music itself, though I'm sure he found the hip-hop style foreign and strange at the time. It was the *message*. It was the language, profane and vulgar; the words dripping with alcohol and littered with drugs; the explicit sexual phrases, the crude debasing of women, and the celebration of a lifestyle of idle hedonism.

There's a fine line between legitimate, uncensored personal expression and the celebration of a violent, sexual lifestyle that's morally bankrupt and destructive. In hip-hop, I often find a music that expresses the frustration and protest I feel inside. But most of the time, hip-hop wallows in a lifestyle that disgusts me, much as it disgusted my father more than two decades ago.

I just wonder what happens when this soundtrack plays in the minds of young black men on the streets of America's cities and towns during times of racial confrontation.

■ ■ ■

These are the lies we tell ourselves:

The lie that hip hop offers "the good life." Some people criticize hip-hop for not being truly authentic, but I don't see a problem with the artists being well compensated for what they do. Even if hip-hop artists who grew up in the hood no longer live there, it doesn't disqualify them from speaking about the ills they once had to face and the injustices they witnessed at one time. I understand that.

I'm frustrated that a lot of hip-hop today seems to misrepresent its original roots in true protest.

But I take issue with the lie that "the good life" is found in large quantities of money, cars, and women. I take issue with what they choose to glorify: pride, self-indulgence, and greed. I take issue with the lie of lyrics that promote what the flesh wants to hear rather than music that sings the truth that people need to hear. I'm frustrated that a lot of hip-hop today seems to misrepresent its original roots in true protest.

I know that hip-hop, like any other genre, affects our minds. And if the pursuit of money, power, and lust (what the Bible calls the lust of the flesh, the lust of the eyes, and the pride of life[3]) is glorified, then those who listen to the music will be drawn to glorify it too—to their detriment. Underneath the so-called good life of hip-hop is the truth about lives based on drugs that ruin our neighborhoods; frivolous sex that destroys the souls of young men and women and leads to a culture of fatherless children; and a preoccupation with money instead of education. These are the lies that tragically undermine young hearts and minds.

The lie that it's cool to treat women badly. The word for the abusive hatred of women is *misogyny*. And hip-hop is drenched in it.

Hip-hop lyrics refer to women as sexual objects, toys, and servants—essentially slaves—in the world of the rich black rapper. Emotional and even physical abuse of women is dominant in hip-hop. While this is obvious to many who are outside that world, it's built into the fabric of hip-hop's message and lyrics, and it's considered a distinctive characteristic of the culture.

I'm deeply frustrated that many people who partake of that culture don't see it and condemn it. Though some do. One black woman speaks volumes in a single paragraph protesting the misogyny of hip-hop.

I'm an African American woman, and if I listened to what hip-hop told me that I was, I'd be the equivalent of nothing. Yesterday's news. Material that must be morphed in order to be worthy. That would be me. Inject manmade material into my God-given body is what they say I should do if I want more "ass-ets." Meanwhile, my curves that derived from Africa, given to me by my creator, should be more than enough. You see, I'd rather have hip-hop appreciate me, being that many of its participants derived from households raised solely by a woman. Prison rates aren't lying to us, and the absence of "fathers" in households is a pretty vivid picture now. How do young black men grow up to spread disrespect toward African American women? Hi, I'm a young black woman, and if I listened to what hip-hop told me I was, I'd be doomed. Defeated. Useless. Paint me another picture, because I'm not buying what hip-hop tells me I am. I am a queen. We started out that way, and we will remain that way.[4]

As a husband, I cannot listen anymore to many of the lyrics of hip-hop and look my wife in the eye. As a father with daughters, I cannot have hip-hop's misogyny in my mind and look my daughters in the eye without fear and trembling about what that culture would do to them. As a father with sons, I am reminded about how my presence and love and example are so important to them growing up, and how hip-hop is the lie I need to protect them from.

The lie that hip-hop is justified in its violence. Again, I respect someone's right to express through books, poetry, or music the true experience of their lives; I respect anyone's honest expression of anger. On the street there is violence, it's rampant, and it's perfectly right for it to be sung about.

I respect someone's honest expression of anger. On the street there is violence, it's rampant, and it's perfectly right for it to be sung about.

Hip-hop specifically tells its fans that cops are bad, are out to harass the innocent, and specifically target black people. I know my friend Chris would argue with me about that, but there is much factual evidence to prove that it's true. I just say to him, "You simply need to know that in the black community, police abuse and brutality are givens. The threat of police to innocent black people is assumed, something everyone knows is true. And the black community knows that the white community is blind to it. Why? *Because they don't experience it.* We do."

So this understanding about life on the streets for the young and black is what hip-hop rants about over and over. As a reflection of truth and reality, I defend hip-hop's right to observe and protest that. As I grew up listening to rap, I found in the lyrics a sound and fury that matched the news of the day—Rodney King being beaten by cops on the streets of LA. The lyrics seemed prophetic and real. So I get it that hip-hop at one time was a reflection of reality.

But hip-hop today contributes to the racial divide by emphasizing violence in response to the problem. Instead of describing experience, it now promotes and prescribes action. Imagine two people entering a confrontation. Let's say one person is in the wrong and knows he's wrong, and the other person calls him out on it. Then clothe one of the people in civilian street clothes and the other in a blue uniform. You have a standoff. Now throw a gun into the mix. See what happens.

This is the story that hip-hop frequently tells. At what point does it go beyond being a reflection of reality and become a trigger for new tragedy?

Hip-hop describes a culture of violence and prescribes an embarrassment of violence.

I'm frustrated because we have believed a lie that says we can listen to, watch, and read about violence, sex, and lawlessness and not expect it to desensitize us. Yet somehow we are surprised when it all continues to play out in the streets. We regurgitate the inequities, poverty, violence, and pain but many times offer no solution. In a twisted way, being put-upon becomes the desired condition of life, and the struggles and even the crimes involved in survival are embraced and glorified. Sadly, it becomes almost preferable to be marginalized because upward mobility is severely limited, along with the hope of things ever getting better.

Sadly, it becomes almost preferable to be marginalized, because upward mobility is severely limited, along with the hope of things ever getting better.

I'm frustrated because I believe hip-hop traps us in our own helplessness.

. . .

I'm frustrated because, despite all of this, I still find myself drawn to hip-hop music. Yeah, I do.

I think that's true for many of us, isn't it? Not just hip-hop but other music—rock, pop, country—as well as movies, television, and video games. We're drawn to our entertainment. Different genres. Same lies. A post on RockWisdom.com states, "Some forms of entertainment clearly undermine the basic foundations of society . . . by acting as a negative and destructive influence. Specific examples are songs that advocate or condone drug use, pornography, racism, gratuitous violence, perversion, religious intolerance, rape, and domestic assaults."[5]

Much of our favorite entertainment, though maybe not in the same way or to the same degree as hip-hop, seems to feature an obsession with violence, a preoccupation with sex, or a self-absorbed focus on "me"—often under a pretense of authenticity and a veneer of art.

NPR interviewed Nathan DeWall, a psychologist from the University of Kentucky who did a study of popular music lyrics. His conclusion was that music in recent years has become much more narcissistic.

What we found over time is that there's an increasing focus on *me* and *my*, instead of *we* and *our* and *us*. . . .

These popular song lyrics are really a mirror of cultural changes in personality, traits, and motivations and emotions. . . .

[Kanye West's music, for example, is] a quintessential example of narcissism, sort of feeling like you really know everything, that you know what's best, that if you don't win awards, it's not that objectively you weren't as good as other people, it's just that people don't really understand how great you are.[6]

Any entertainment that exalts the self inherently feeds pride, and pride is the biggest problem that leads to violence and death. Self is exalted in movies and music when women are portrayed as objects to be used for pleasure, and are depicted as always willing and wanting to please any man in any way at any time. Self is exalted in movies and music when love of money is honored as the most important mission and accumulation of wealth is seen as more important than relationships. Self is exalted by musicians and filmmakers who are so self-absorbed that they can hardly create something about anyone but themselves. Ultimately, it is all about self. And pride.

On the streets, it's pride that fuels the escalation of violence—whether it's the pride of the detained refusing to cooperate or the pride of the officer ignoring protocol and forcing submission.

The problem of race in America is within us. It's not "out there." It's inside here.

The problem of race in America is within us. It's not "out there." It's inside here.

· · ·

I think about my father's disgust on that fateful day when I came home from school to find him holding the Snoop Dogg cassette. It wasn't just the vulgar lyrics that he wanted out of his house, although that was a major part of it. In his wisdom, he knew how powerfully captivating music was and that my being captivated at a young age by what was on that tape could lead me into a life of reckless behavior that might possibly get me killed. He knew that this music would not walk me toward my greatest potential but would trap me in a cycle of lowest expectations. He knew it would not motivate me to work and achieve but would sedate me in a life of idleness and anger.

And things were no different across town in the white neighborhoods. Maybe over there it wasn't hip-hop, exactly, but there was still the downward drag of popular cultural norms that glorify rebellion, sex, and violence. I know that my father would have hoped that his white counterpart was doing the same thing—correcting and motivating his son to aim higher, embrace good, and do what's right. Otherwise, the mind of the white father's son was as fertile as mine was for seeds of bias, planted through media messages of violence, long before the white son would someday pull me over at a traffic stop.

. . .

Today my father is a pastor in South Carolina.

I don't know what music he listened to as a kid, but I know he watched TV because he saw the Billy Graham crusade broadcast that changed his life. When he talks about getting saved, I know how he means that in the spiritual sense, but in another way I think he knows he was also saved from one way of life into a different way of life—and maybe literally saved from an early death. And that difference has meant everything in his view of race and the course of his life since then.

Holiness is a word we don't use much anymore . . . [but] it's a word that has a lot to do with how we live our lives.

I think that's a choice we all have.

Not long ago, my dad preached a sermon on holiness. *Holiness* is a word we don't use much anymore. We usually associate it with religion and being a pastor, a priest, a monk, or a nun in a church, monastery, or convent. We assume it's not for us, and we easily dismiss it.

In fact, it's a word that has a lot to do with how we live our lives.

Understanding holiness involves a comparison to God, one in which we as human beings inevitably fall short. But *holiness* also carries the meaning of "living with a highly moral or spiritual purpose." It suggests that there is something important in aiming higher, embracing what is good, and trying to do what's right.

Holiness is a word we don't use much anymore.

And it's not a word you'll ever find in hip-hop.

FEARFUL AND CONFUSED

I'M FEARFUL

because in the back of my mind I know that although I'm a law-abiding citizen, I could still be looked upon as a "threat" to those who don't know me. So I will continue to have to go the extra mile to earn the benefit of the doubt.

I'M CONFUSED

because I don't know why it's so hard to obey a policeman. You will not win!!! And I don't know why some policemen abuse their power. Power is a responsibility, not a weapon to brandish and lord over the populace.

I REMEMBER HELPING my laboring wife into our white Range Rover around 3 a.m. on a bone-crunching cold morning in January 2009. Her mom was with us, which gave me some comfort, but this would be our first child, and I admit I was nervous. Though I had done the homework every prospective dad does to prepare the necessary provisions and transportation for the trip to the hospital, my mind was filled with TV shows I'd seen in which the father-to-be has everything in order for the fateful moment, then walks out the door forgetting only one thing—his pregnant wife. So I was determined not to forget Kirsten for the morning run to the hospital.

We were living in Boston at the time. I had just finished my fifth year with the New England Patriots, a year that had proven disappointing for the team. Quarterback Tom Brady had been injured in the first quarter of the first game of the season, tearing his ACL and MCL and needing surgery and a year of recovery. Backup QB Matt Cassel stepped in and did a remarkable job leading us to a strong 11–5 record in the regular season. Unfortunately, it wasn't quite enough to get us into the playoffs: the only time we would fail to make the postseason in all my years there.

Of course, none of this mattered to Kirsten, her mom, or me as we drove that morning. It matters only in context: This was Super Bowl weekend, and this year I was not playing in the big game.

I remember thinking two things in the car that night. One

was that it would be funny if, on this particular night, I would get pulled over. That's the running joke on so many black sitcoms on TV: "Why are you late getting home from work?" "I got pulled over." So getting pulled over would be funny—not in a ha-ha way but in an "of course" way. As I slid behind the wheel, I vowed to be careful to keep it under the speed limit—despite the urgency—and drive between the lines. At 3 a.m., there wouldn't be much traffic. I'd be okay.

My only other thought was about Kirsten.

.   .   .

The first time I ever saw Kirsten was at a block party next to the student center at the University of Georgia. It was an opportunity for students to mingle at the beginning of the school year. I remember she was wearing red pants and a white blouse with a collar, and she looked so classy, elegant, and incredibly striking. I couldn't help but notice.

The first time I ever saw Kirsten was at a block party. . . . She looked so classy, elegant, and incredibly striking. I couldn't help but notice.

I don't know if she noticed me that day, but I soon had some help in getting her attention—from Janie Jones, the wife of one of the football coaches. A white woman with a big heart for students white and black, Miss Janie was beloved by everybody. Through the Fellowship of Christian Athletes, she happened to have a connection to my dad and to Kirsten. Miss Janie had incredible energy and enthusiasm, and to many of us at school she was an encourager, a counselor, and a friend.

And a matchmaker.

Miss Janie, it turned out, was telling Kirsten to ditch her current boyfriend and get with me. Likewise, Miss Janie played

Cupid by telling me that Kirsten was really the right woman for me. Our first "date" was at the Snelling Dining Hall at UGA, but we stayed "just friends" for quite a while.

Miss Janie would say it was just a matter of time, though some who knew Kirsten and me weren't quite so certain. For one thing, she and I argued and fought a lot. Both of us are strong-willed firstborns, and we had to negotiate our space and establish our turf with each other. I was always messing up and having to apologize. One time after Kirsten and I had a fight about something, I realized later that I was just plain wrong. I showed up at her place wearing a T-shirt on which I'd written, "Will you forgive me?" Although she was still really steamed with me, seeing my homemade T-shirt prompted a slow smile on Kirsten's face.

I had never met anyone like her.

We graduated together, with Kirsten earning a degree in marketing while mine was in finance. I stayed at UGA for another year to play football with the Bulldogs, but Kirsten moved to Atlanta to take a job at the corporate offices of Home Depot. She drove over to Athens on game days to watch me play. The management-training program took Kirsten to LA, while I landed in Boston after being drafted by the Patriots.

We were now three thousand miles apart, and I knew I had to make a decision. I confess, I was apprehensive about the future. My friends would ask, "Why are you scared?" I didn't know. I was just afraid and indecisive. Was I going to commit to Kirsten, or would I let her go? Kirsten was talking about traveling abroad, exploring career options around the world. And she was not one to wait around. She knew what she was worth, and she thought I was worth it too; but she wasn't going to hang around until I figured things out. She wanted her man to commit. If not, she'd move on.

As I say, I'd never met anyone like her.

It came down to this—I knew I needed her in my life. Sometimes you get to that point, and you just know something. Though it took me a while, I got there. And then I *knew*.

I set about buying a ring, but I couldn't decide which one. So I bought two.

I made plans to go to Kirsten's parents and ask them for her hand in marriage. As nervous as I could possibly be, I approached them and managed to squeeze out the words: "I'm asking your permission to marry your daughter."

Her dad looked at me without expression. He paused. And then with utmost gravity and seriousness he said, "If you hurt my Pookie, I'll bust a cap in your butt."

Okay. I wasn't sure if that was a yes, but I believed he would do what he said.

I proposed to Kirsten one perfect evening at a resort in Santa Barbara. Well, the evening was perfect, but I was a mess. I was nervous, clumsy, acting weird. I'd planned to have some music playing in the background, but I couldn't get the boom box to play. Nothing else was going right.

But eventually, I got down on one knee and said, "Kirsten, will you marry me?"

She smiled and said, "Yes."

Relieved, I reached into my pocket. "I didn't know which ring to get you, so I got you two."

■　■　■

Now I was driving through Boston at three in the morning, a little frantic to get to the hospital but being especially careful not to go over the speed limit. Still, I was apprehensive. When you're black, you know it doesn't matter if you keep to the speed limit and stay within the lines.

I looked over at Kirsten, who was doing fine but was clearly ready to give birth to our child. I saw the ring she was wearing, which was neither of the two I had picked out. I remembered my nervousness when I had proposed, and I was nervous now, but in a different way. I just needed to get us—the three of us—to the hospital without delay.

I was apprehensive. When you're black, you know it doesn't matter if you keep to the speed limit and stay within the lines.

I pulled onto the interstate. In Boston, where space is at a premium, a lot of the highways have short on-ramps and merging lanes. But thankfully, there was little traffic, and I managed to pull the Range Rover into the rightmost lane. Good. Things would be okay.

Within minutes, I was pulled over by a cop.

■   ■   ■

White people have no idea of the fear that black people feel toward the police. I cannot say that strongly enough, loudly enough, or forcefully enough. I believe it is a *huge* point of division between black people and white people. Black people have little expectation of being treated fairly by police in any situation. We have a high expectation of being demeaned, abused, and possibly treated violently in any encounter with law enforcement. We have a history that supports this, news headlines that shout this, and personal experiences that confirm this.

This is a reality that white people simply don't know.

My friend Chris says, "I don't get it. Why does so-and-so run when they're pulled over? If they're innocent, they'll be fine."

"You're right, you *don't* get it," I say. "It doesn't matter if you're innocent. If you're black, there's a very different set of assumptions. We believe that cops overall have a bias against black people, that we are more likely to be singled out, and that we can be innocent and yet run into trouble at the hands of the cops."

Pew Research Center documents this belief in a recent poll "in which blacks expressed far less confidence than whites in local police to treat both races equally."[1] The *Wall Street Journal* echoes these findings: "The racial split is even greater on the question of whether the police treat whites and blacks equally, the poll found. Some 69 percent of white voters expressed confidence that law enforcement officials gave equal treatment to people of both races, while just 28 percent of black voters held that view."[2]

But black people don't need statistics to know the truth of our perceptions. Many of us have felt the fear of being stopped by cops or of the possibility of being pulled over as we've seen done to others. There is a fear of physical harm, of demeaning treatment and unjust accusations, and of the complicated legal process that might ensue. When there is even a threat of the police becoming involved, we act in certain fearful ways. This is the reality that white people don't know.

> When there is even a threat of the police becoming involved, we act in certain fearful ways. This is the reality that white people don't know.

Journalist Nikole Hannah-Jones tells of going with her family to Long Island to visit some friends over the Fourth of July one year. After dinner, they decided to walk along the beach and boardwalk.

Most of the foot traffic was heading in one direction, but then two teenage girls came toward us, moving stiffly against the flow, both of them looking nervously to their right. "He's got a gun," one of them said in a low voice.

I turned my gaze to follow theirs, and was clasping my four-year-old daughter's hand when a young man

extended his arm and fired off multiple shots along the
busy street running parallel to the boardwalk. Snatching
my daughter up into my arms, I joined the throng of
screaming revelers running away from the gunfire and
toward the water.[3]

After the shooting stopped and Hannah-Jones determined that
everyone in her group was safe, she noticed that one of her com-
panions, a young high school intern who was visiting, was on the
phone.

Unable to imagine whom she would be calling at that
moment, I asked her, somewhat indignantly, if she couldn't
have waited until we got to safety before calling her mom.
"No," she said. "I am talking to the police."
My friends and I locked eyes in stunned silence.
Between the four adults, we hold six degrees. Three of us
are journalists. And not one of us had thought to call the
police. We had not even considered it.
We also are all black. And without realizing it, in that
moment, each of us had made a set of calculations, an
instantaneous weighing of the pros and cons. . . .
Calling the police posed considerable risks. It carried
the very real possibility of inviting disrespect, even physical harm. We had seen witnesses treated like suspects, and
knew how quickly black people calling the police for help
could wind up cuffed in the back of a squad car. Some of
us knew of black professionals who'd had guns drawn on
them for no reason.[4]

The young intern, who was biracial, was interrogated by phone
four times by the cops. *Four times.* At one point, she was asked,

"Are you really trying to be helpful, or were you involved in this?" Now much more aware of the trend of the questions, she asked the others in the group, "Are they going to come get me?"

One of the other women said, "See, that's why we don't call them."[5]

When I told him this, my friend Chris nodded, but he pushed back a little.

"I can understand why some people would be apprehensive after the recent events in Ferguson and elsewhere. These tragedies might raise that specter of fear."

"Yes," I said. "But this incident happened *before* Ferguson and these other recent tragedies. And that's my point—black people have for a long time borne the fear of those in power. This is not new."

This is the reality that white people don't know.

I told Chris about my own recent experience. Kirsten and I were out on a date night, having had a fabulous dinner at a nearby restaurant. Driving home, we wound our way through the city and drove down one street where, up ahead, we could see state troopers out in force, looking in car windows and checking driver's registrations. I didn't know what was up, but the intensity of the police presence was unusual. I felt panicked. I had nothing to hide, nothing but a valid license and registration to show. And yet I was fearful. I didn't want to be put in a precarious situation with the cops or to encounter an officer who was simply having a bad day. Especially with Kirsten in the car, I didn't want trouble. The thought of any number of unfolding scenarios, none of them good, filled my head—and I started to plan my escape. I quickly calculated how I might turn ahead and slide out on a side street to avoid the scrutiny of the cops. As it turned out, there was no alternative route, and I had no choice but to continue driving through the gauntlet of law enforcement.

I wonder what might have happened if I had been able to turn, and the cops had seen me veer off and decided to apprehend me. Even though I was innocent, my every instinct was to try to get away. I know that my inclination to run might very well have been what could have created a major incident. All of this was based on my assumption that, in getting stopped by the cops, I would likely not get a fair deal because I am black.

> Even though I was innocent, my every instinct was to try to get away. I know that my inclination to run might very well have been what could have created a major incident.

I continued to drive along the street and made it through. No one stopped us. Relief set in, but it was short lived. Abruptly, a car's high beams reflected off my rearview mirror, making me squint, and the sound of voices could be heard close by. I honestly thought about speeding away and claiming ignorance later. But I didn't, and it turned out to be nothing. We passed through and made our way home without incident.

"Chris," I said. "This is *me* we're talking about. I had done nothing wrong. I am a successful person with a degree in finance and a career in professional football. I had no reason to respond that way. Yet I did. I responded like that because I had no expectation that I would be treated well by a cop, and I had every expectation that something bad would go down. That is the black experience."

It would be funny if it weren't so sobering.

Kirsten tells the story of when she was in high school, driving home from a church function with two of her friends, both black. They got pulled over by a cop. There was no reason for the stop, other than the cop's suspicion.

"Why are you driving in a neighborhood you have no business in?" he asked.

"Because I live here," Kirsten replied.

The officer had pulled her over right in front of her house.

There are thousands of black experiences like this. Stories of innocent black people who are stopped for no good reason or on the assumption that they're in a neighborhood where they don't belong. There is good reason for black people to have a wary view of the police.

Historian Heather Ann Thompson, a professor at Temple University, writes about twentieth-century urban politics. Commenting on Ferguson, she says,

> It's much more about the fact that there is an absolute
> unwillingness to deal with the core issues in American
> society about equality in the streets: [the principle that]
> a black citizen and a white citizen really do have equal
> rights under the laws. Black citizens don't believe it. They
> shouldn't believe it. It's not true that they have equal
> rights under the laws. It's not true that they have the same
> assumptions of innocence. It's not true that they have the
> same assumptions of peaceful countenance.[6]

I know Chris has a low tolerance for black history, but I couldn't help but refer to it. It's part of the equation. I have no doubt that mistrust of the police stems from the earliest days of emancipation, when hope and freedom were turned into fear and dread as judicial systems attempted to reinstate "order," essentially kidnapping and enslaving thousands of black men, forcing them to work in conditions that were in many ways worse than chattel slavery.

Douglas Blackmon tells one such story of Green Cottenham, a black man arrested for a concocted charge of vagrancy, sentenced to hard labor, and *sold* in 1908 (long after emancipation) to the US Steel Corporation for a year of hard labor in a coal mine.

The [labor] camp had supplied tens of thousands of men over five decades to a succession of prison mines ultimately purchased by US Steel in 1907. Hundreds of them had not survived. Nearly all were black men arrested and then "leased" by state and county governments to US Steel or the companies it had acquired.

Here and in scores of other similarly crude graveyards, the final chapter of American slavery had been buried. It was a form of bondage distinctly different from that of the antebellum South in that for most men, and the relatively few women drawn in, this slavery did not last a lifetime and did not automatically extend from one generation to the next. But it was nonetheless slavery—a system in which armies of free men, guilty of no crimes and entitled by law to freedom, were compelled to labor without compensation, were repeatedly bought and sold, and were forced to do the bidding of white masters through the regular application of extraordinary physical coercion.[7]

This was the United States justice system supplying forced black labor to corporate America long after slavery had been abolished. So how can we trust the power structure of white politics and white law enforcement to have our best interests in mind?

But it's more specific than that. There is a history of black people literally being hunted down like animals and pursued as targets by lynch mobs, the KKK, and local police.

The 1923 massacre at Rosewood, a small town in Florida, is one case in point. A black man was accused of raping a white woman. A lynching party of about twenty or thirty white people set out one night to hunt him down. The search for the accused became a hunt as well for "accomplices" and family who might be harboring him. In short order, many black people were killed, the entire town of predominantly black families was burned to the ground, and any survivors fled into the nearby swamps. It was later determined that the white woman who had claimed she was raped was likely covering for her affair with a different man, who was white.

Using black slaves as targets was a common carnival game and circus act for white entertainment in the late nineteenth and early twentieth centuries. I'm talking about aiming at and hitting real live people in the head with baseballs. It was called African Dodger, and it persisted into the 1920s, when black masks were substituted for the heads and faces of real human beings.[8]

> The notion of being targeted and pursued are matters that are deeply sensitive for black people, as they echo a history that is shameful, demeaning, and abusive.

So, the notion of being targeted and pursued is a matter that is deeply sensitive for black people, as it echoes a history that is shameful, demeaning, and abusive.

Of course, "that was back then," some might say. Why dwell on it now?

Because it wasn't really just *back then*.

A group of ten young white people—*ten* of them—intentionally hunted down black people in Jackson, Mississippi, firing slingshots and throwing beer bottles at them. One such black man, James Craig Anderson, was hunted down, attacked, and then run over with a truck. You might think this happened in the early 1900s. It happened in 2011.[9]

Many Americans have seen the tragic video of Walter Scott, a black man who was stopped for a missing taillight and wound up dead. While the officer, Michael Slager, was at his patrol car performing a license check, Scott ran from the scene, and Slager pursued him on foot. And then, in a scene captured in a bystander video, Slager, incredibly, raised his gun and fired eight shots at Scott, hitting him in the back and killing him.

At the vigil for Walter Scott, state representative Wendell Gilliard spoke powerfully about the context for the tragedy:

> Young black men, unarmed, are being hunted down like deer. The sound that you hear on that film, I get that sound all the time traveling back and forth from Charleston to Columbia. Everybody would tell me, "Don't get excited, Representative, because it's deer hunting season." That young man was hunted down like a deer, like so many other black men in our country. This is not a North Charleston problem. This is not a Charleston problem. This is America's problem, and we have yet to resolve the issue.[10]

This is not about back then. This is about right now.

This is about Tamir Rice, a twelve-year-old boy who was shot while holding a BB gun. This is about John Crawford III, who was shot dead inside a Walmart store because he was holding a pellet gun that was on sale there. This is about Eric Garner, who was choked to death by police. This is about Jonathan Ferrell, who knocked on someone's door for help after a late-night auto accident. After the homeowner, fearing a break-in, called the police, they responded and ended up shooting Ferrell ten times, killing him. This is about Amadou Diallo, who was killed while holding his wallet, shot at forty-one times (and struck nineteen times) "because he fit the general description" of a wanted serial rapist.[11] This is about Michael Brown, who was shot six times for—well, we don't know.

A website lists these and many more deaths that are similar—some seventy-six people of color killed by police between

1999 and 2014. These are only the ones we know about. The comments section on the website is still open for posting more tragic killings when they happen.[12]

But aren't there accounts of white people shot by police as well?

Yes, and I think that's tragic too. If cops are doing these things to *anyone*, we should *all* be up in arms.

. . .

Yes, I think we could talk more about all those people, black *and* white, who have been assaulted or killed by police. This is heartbreaking for all of us.

But my point is that there is a perception among black people—supported by a lot of history, current events, and reality—that leads to deep fear when it comes to law enforcement. My point is that this is *the* great divide between black people and white people today. My point is that a white person might think he or she understands this but likely does not. My point is that a black person and a white person feel differently, act differently, and respond differently when a cop approaches.

So there is perception. But what is reality? Do the facts support the fear?

This is currently the national debate, with pundits from the left and the right arguing about what is true. Conservatives point to one set of statistics, proving there is no racism; liberals use a different set of numbers to say that racism is obviously rampant. And once again we have talking heads in a shouting match, each trying to win by force of volume, each wanting to convince us that what they believe is true.

I could quote statistics that I believe are solid and true—for example, that black teens are twenty-one times more likely to be shot dead by police than white teens are.[13] I could cite a report that shows how the police in Ferguson for a long time have had a clear bias against blacks in the community.[14] I can mention statistics showing that blacks and whites use marijuana at nearly the same rate, yet blacks are arrested four times more often than whites for marijuana possession.[15]

Yet I know that others would cite statistics from their own sources that would suggest a different story. So we continue to find ourselves heading to our respective corners.

No matter whom you listen to, the core problem is that there is no comprehensive clearinghouse in America that captures all the data or even enough data to be meaningful. Many statistics come from the FBI database, which the agency itself admits is woefully incomplete. Additionally, homicides by police are notoriously underreported—we simply don't know everything that has happened. And then the significance of all the statistics must be meticulously *interpreted*—how much has to do with poverty, how much with race, how much with crime? How much information is left out when quoting our statistics and drawing our conclusions?

We know that more white people than black people are killed by cops, but there are five times more whites than blacks in the US. And even when you look at the percentages of whites versus blacks killed by police, that still isn't the full story. You have to look at the location and scope of the data. I have no problem conceding that the percentage of white people killed by cops in, say, Bozeman, Montana, is greater than the percentage of blacks killed there. And I don't think you can compare the statistics from mixed-race towns and cities like Ferguson, Missouri, to those from upscale white suburbs around the country.

Much is made of black-on-black crime—the common assertion that a high percentage of black people commit crimes against other blacks. But what is often left out are statistics about white-on-white crime, which is equally high. The fact is, we are largely a segregated society, and thus crimes committed in our segregated communities will more likely be committed against members of our own race.

> Much is made of black-on-black crime. . . . But what is often left out are statistics about white-on-white crime, which is equally high.

With my background in finance, I understand the value of numbers. I don't want to dismiss statistics completely, but I'm well aware that statistics can *appear* to say one thing and yet actually say something else. I know that the truth of many statistics lies far deeper than the talking heads and politicians ever care to dig. And that truth can swing to one side or the other of the racial divide.

I suggest that we should be careful with statistics thrown around in the media, and I suggest that we be careful to base our protests on truth. That goes for both whites and blacks, but maybe for black people especially. If the real and true statistics in a certain situation do *not* show police bias or targeting, we need to face and accept that truth honestly.

I suggest that we challenge the claims made by certain celebrities, commentators, and politicians wielding half-truth statistics that "there is no racism." To say that is ignorant. And, in itself, racist.

I suggest that we all try to get beyond the statistics and agree together that the unjust killing of *any* person by the police is a tragedy.

Can't we see in the deaths of those who have been killed—white and black—the tragedy of a lost life? Can't we reach out to one another and grieve together? Can't we find at least that one place in common, that place of love and loss, where we can be human together?

■ ■ ■

I'm confused, because I don't know why it's so hard to obey a policeman. You will not win!!! And I don't know why some policemen abuse their power. Power is a responsibility, not a weapon to brandish and lord over the populace.

I wrote this statement on my Facebook page the night of the Ferguson decision, with my emotions flowing out of my fatherhood. It was a desperate cry to those young men, sons of fathers, to understand: This is the world you are in. For your own sake and for the sake of life itself, I beg you: Just do what the man in blue says. Let go of your fear, your rage, and your defiance for just one moment in order to live another day.

I know that your every instinct is to run, as it was for me that one night driving through New Orleans. But ultimately there's only one thing to do. And that is to do what the policeman says.

Upon reflection, I understand one problem with what I wrote that night. It's the word *obey*. Obedience is what masters once required of their slaves. After the Civil War, obedience by black people was built into the Black Codes: laws applying only to blacks that limited their freedoms and became essentially another form of slavery. Obedience echoes the separate-but-equal requirements of the segregation era. Obedience smacks of the harsh commands to black people by Southern cops in the 1960s.

To black people, *obey* is a loaded word.

Some radical factions in the black community have called for black people never to obey "the white man's law." In an interview on CNN with Anderson Cooper, New Black Panther Party spokesman Minister Mikhail Muhammad said, "I don't obey the white man's law, I don't follow the American law. The American law—the American law does not protect me, Anderson. I'm not a citizen. So I have no right to respect American law."[16]

I don't believe that, of course, and neither do most black American citizens. But the feeling and attitude toward the command to *obey* is deeply entrenched. Being told to obey—especially to obey white authority—is as offensive as anything to young black men and women who struggle for respect and dignity in a culture of poverty and challenge.

Much has been made of the Bible's commands to slaves to obey their masters. And those verses were indeed used by slave owners to convince slaves that their plight was divine in origin and that any rebellion would be a rebellion against God himself.

The Bible explicitly condemns kidnapping, which was at the center of the transatlantic African slave trade.

Although the Bible does speak to slaves, admonishing them toward obedience with sincerity of heart, it also instructs masters to treat justly the slaves under their control, showing them goodwill and concern. Clearly, many American slave masters skipped over that part of the verse.

And though slavery was a practice in the culture of Bible times, it is often misunderstood as being the same as what was practiced in America. The Bible explicitly condemns kidnapping, which was at the center of the transatlantic African slave trade.[17] Furthermore, much of slavery in biblical times was economic, not racial. People sold themselves into indentured servitude for a specified time when debts could not be paid, choosing to serve their master so that the basic needs of their family for food, clothing, and shelter could be met.[18] It was not the dehumanizing, forced racial slavery that was institutionalized in early American history.

But the language of slavery and obedience in the Bible can affect a black person differently than a white person. Recently, a popular white Christian blogger, Rachel Held Evans, wrote online about her error at a recent speaking engagement:

> I ran headlong into my own "sincere ignorance and conscientious stupidity" just two weeks ago when I gave a lecture for a writers conference at Princeton Theological Seminary and in reference to Jesus' parable of the vineyard workers, described God as a "generous master" whom we serve with our faithful work. Afterwards, a black woman approached me and with far more grace than I deserved, reminded me that to African American listeners like her the image of God as a cosmic master is not only discomforting but frightening and oppressive.[19]

Evans apologizes for using that imagery. I don't blame her, and I appreciate her candidness. But it speaks to a reality that white people don't know. It speaks to the association between the words *obedience*, *master*, and *slave* that many white people never intend but that black people struggle with.

Now, I don't believe that the answer is for everyone to tiptoe around their word choices. We already have enough political correctness confusing the real issues. But I understand the problem we have with the word *obey*. And I guess I really do understand why it's so hard to *obey* a policeman.

But here's a reality that many black people don't know: Somehow, some way, we have to *get over it*. We have to suck it up and obey when we are called to. We really must learn the practical value of obeying a policeman, if only to save our own skins sometimes. Otherwise, we will not win.

I think the bigger problem today is the lack of respect for authority in general. Disobeying a police officer is only the tip of the iceberg. Some men and women who would defy a police officer are the same ones who bristle at instructions from their bosses at work. They are the ones who wouldn't listen to the teacher at school and who have hamstrung today's education system with few disciplinary options.

My sister, a teacher, laments the difficult time she has at school when kids are unruly and when parents seem to assume their kid could never do anything wrong. The root of this defiance is kindled in the home, where many parents, of all shades and ethnicities, are absent, detached, or simply defeated when it comes to instilling respect for authority into their children.

I understand that, for many black people, it's hard to obey white authority. It's counterintuitive to obey someone who we think is out to harm us.

We live in an increasingly self-centered culture where, more and more, "we" is becoming "me." This plays out before our very eyes when we refuse to be told what to do and how to act and we preach that individuals should do what's best for them. The problem is that what's best for us is not always what we think is best for us.

But I do understand that, for many black people, it's hard to obey white authority. It's counterintuitive to obey someone who we think is out to harm us. Law enforcement officers have gotten a reputation for mistreating people of color—and as we've seen, some of that reputation is deserved. So I understand—and I feel in myself—the adrenaline of the confrontation with someone we suspect may be out to harm us.

But this is unfortunate. I also believe that the majority of police officers are on our side, making it their life's work to protect and serve us.

So the question remains: How can I call black men and women to obey a police officer? How can I beg our people not to run?

Because I'm a father. Because I fear you will not win. Because I really don't know why some policemen abuse their power. Because I believe that, nine times out of ten, if you run, you will be shot. Because I believe you have a better chance of surviving if you obey.

"The cultural disconnect is very real; you have the weight of generations of abuse on African Americans," says Cincinnati police chief Jeffrey Blackwell, who is black. "My father told me, 'Put your hands up if you encounter a police officer.' I have that same fear for my own son, unfortunately."[20]

Responding to all the violence we've seen in the last few years against black people, a close friend and former NFL player called me, emotionally torn over these tragedies. He lamented, "I tell my son, 'Just do whatever the officers tell you. I don't care if they're right or not. I want to see you alive. Daddy has money for bail and we will figure it out later.'"

So this is what I will tell my children when they are older. I will say, "Obey the cops. I know that will be something you fear. I know there are stories of black people for whom it didn't end well. I know that your instinct will be to run, but don't."

I imagine one of them protesting, "But that's not fair."

"No, it isn't," I will reply.

"Why do we have to do all that stuff?"

"Because you're black. Because this is the world we have."

. . .

I realize that I never finished the story about the birth of our first child. So let me close the chapter with that conclusion.

My wife, her mother, and I were stopped by the side of the interstate at three o'clock in the morning. And by now, Kirsten was in full labor.

The white cop who had pulled us over took some time in his patrol car before opening his door. To avoid any passing traffic on the very narrow shoulders of the Boston interstate, he walked slowly in front of his squad car to the passenger side of our SUV. Leaning in, he asked for my license and registration.

I pulled it out and handed it over.

I asked why we'd been stopped. He didn't answer.

"Where are you goin'?" he asked.

"The hospital. We're about to have a baby."

I had a brief moment during which I recalled TV shows I'd seen where the cops pulled out in front of the expecting couple's car and led the way with lights flashing as a police escort to the hospital. I was hoping he'd be a hero.

But that didn't happen. The cop shone his flashlight on Kirsten's pregnant belly. He paused. He checked my registration and license one more time before handing them back through the open window.

"Get there, then," he said gruffly.

And he walked away.

I don't think there was any cause for us being pulled over. He never gave us one. In thinking about it later, I don't remember if he had previously tailed us or had pulled alongside our car before stopping us. It was such a strange encounter. Even more surreal at 3 a.m.

But it didn't matter.

We got to the hospital in time. Hours later, Kirsten gave birth. Our beautiful baby girl entered the world we have.

God had been good to me. I was a lucky guy to have married Kirsten. I was now a lucky father of a precious daughter.

Her name is Grace.

SAD AND SYMPATHETIC

I'M SAD

*because another young life was lost from his family;
the racial divide has widened; a community is
in shambles; accusations, insensitivity, hurt, and
hatred are boiling over; and we may never know
the truth about what happened that day.*

I'M SYMPATHETIC

*because I wasn't there, so I don't know exactly
what happened. Maybe Darren Wilson acted within
his rights and duty as an officer of the law and
killed Michael Brown in self-defense like any of us
would in the circumstance. Now he has to fear the
backlash against himself and his loved ones when
he was only doing his job. What a horrible thing
to endure. Or maybe he provoked Michael and
ignited the series of events that led to his eventually
murdering the young man to prove a point.*

THE FILM *A TIME TO KILL*, based on a book by John Grisham, tells a fictional, modern-day story of a racial crime in a small Mississippi town. A ten-year-old black girl, Tonya Hailey, is picked up by two young white supremacists, who rape, beat, and subsequently try to hang her. Remarkably, she survives, and the two men are arrested.

The girl's dad, Carl Lee Hailey (powerfully portrayed by Samuel L. Jackson), seeks the counsel of liberal lawyer Jake Brigance (Matthew McConaughey). Brigance tells Hailey that, without better evidence, the two men will go free; he recalls another case years earlier when four white men raped a black girl and were acquitted. Hailey takes matters into his own hands and shoots the two perpetrators on the courthouse steps.

Now Carl Lee Hailey is the one apprehended, jailed, and soon to go on trial.

One of the interesting messages of the film comes through the lawyer, Jake Brigance. Many might recognize a piece of themselves in his character. A civil rights lawyer, Jake is a young, slick hotshot, but he has a driving passion to defend black people's rights in the South. For him, racial injustice is an issue he can do battle with in court, and he loves the challenge. Yet as the film progresses, we become aware that his passion is intellectual and conceptual, not personal.

The lawyer's opponent in court is a redneck district attorney, Rufus Buckley, played by Kevin Spacey. The state is seeking the death penalty for Hailey. Brigance is denied a change of venue—Hailey will be tried in the very town where the two men he shot had lived. This is the "new" South, a place where racial equality is mouthed but injustices and racial violence are acted out on the side and in the dark. In the film and in the book, this is Mississippi, but it could be Anywhere, America. It could be Ferguson.

Ellen Roark (played by Sandra Bullock), a lawyer from the North with experience in death penalty cases, flies in to help. She and Brigance pursue their passion for civil rights together in preparing to defend Carl Lee Hailey in court.

The KKK, in the dark of night, harasses the defense team. At first, it's bomb threats and cross burnings. Then they burn down Brigance's house. Later, they kidnap and torture Roark, leaving her tied to a stake in the woods. She is rescued, but the defense lawyers are rattled and scared.

The jury, it's determined, is leaning heavily toward finding Carl Lee Hailey guilty.

What interests me is the relationship between Carl and Jake. Even though Jake represents Carl's interests, Carl sees through that. He calls Jake on it: "Nigger, Negro, black, African American—no matter how you see me, you see me as different. You see me like that jury sees me. You are them." Carl knows that Jake is committed to a case, not a person. Jake is a lawyer, not his friend. Jake embraces a passion for a legal win but not a relationship with the man he is defending.

In a powerful scene, Carl tells him: "We are on different sides of the line. I ain't never seen you in my part of town. I bet you don't even know where I live. Our daughters, Jake, they ain't never gonna play together."[1]

This being a John Grisham story, the final act ends in a dramatic courtroom scene. The arguments go back and forth, and Carl's fate looks more and more bleak. But Jake Brigance prepares a speech for his final argument. It's considered one of the great movie speeches of all time.

What *A Time to Kill* illustrates, I believe, is the difference between the *issues* we hold dear and the *people* we hold dear. It shows what happens when people—black and white—are jolted out of a distant view of the "other side" and into a close-up view of real people on that side. It depicts the power of the human heart—if we just allow the human heart to become engaged.

In the final scene, Carl Lee Hailey, now acquitted, is outside with dozens of neighborhood friends and families. It's a picnic barbecue to celebrate his acquittal.

A car pulls up. Out steps a white family—Jake Brigance; his wife; and his daughter, Hannah. They walk up to Carl and his wife. The two wives exchange hellos. Hannah is introduced to Carl's daughter, Tonya.

Jake and Carl face each other, both realizing they've been through the gauntlet together yet still don't really know each other. They look at each other for some moments, both grim-faced.

Jake breaks the silence: "I just thought our kids might play together."

Carl nods slightly. And then a faint smile spreads across his face.

So many, like Jake Brigance, posture a passion for equal rights and justice. And yet while they embrace their intellectual passion, they keep their personal connection to real people at arm's length. This is the problem. We are separate. We keep ourselves separate. Even those who make a show of sympathy for racial issues keep separate from the people who live in it. We don't look for ways to personally connect with each other.

Our children don't play together.

The story of *A Time to Kill* is not, for me, so much about a courtroom drama or the depiction of racial injustice. For me, it's about a white man with the best of liberal intentions coming to the realization that he has to allow it to become personal.

. . .

One of the things that fuels racism is *numbers*. And the safety we find in them.

When we're in our peer groups—shooting the breeze with a group of buddies, hanging out with coworkers after work, meeting with couples from church, attending a small group in the neighborhood—we tend to blend in with the attitudes and assumptions of those around us. Someone says something judgmental, another chimes in, and eventually someone else says something to top what the first person said. Who are we to disagree? Soon there is a consensus of opinion in our group about another group.

One of the things that fuels racism is *numbers*. And the safety we find in them.

Black or white, the groups we're in tend to confirm the worst of the biases and judgmentalism we harbor inside ourselves.

When we as races are separate, safe among the numbers of white people or black people surrounding us, we lose sight of the others' humanity.

We lose sight of the fact that each of us is a son or daughter and that the person we're judging out there is also a son or daughter. We lose sight of the fact that there are mothers and fathers on both sides. Is it possible for a white mother and a black mother to find their common humanity in the fact that they are both mothers, rather than as members of groups that spew their prejudices based on the difference of being black or white?

If I, a black man, am with you, a white man, and together we are watching our sons play in the yard, am I not more inclined to see you as a father rather than as a white man? And are you not more inclined to see me as a father rather than as a black man? It seems more likely that our conversation will begin to flow as we talk about our sons and who they are and what they did in baseball, rather than getting stuck in a halting, stilted conversation about the racial issues that divide us.

But we are separate. We remain incredibly segregated. So we don't sit down together at neighborhood picnics. We don't hang out together after work. We don't worship together in our churches.

At the beginning of his closing argument in *A Time to Kill*, Jake Brigance says:

> I set out to prove a black man could receive a fair trial
> in the South—that we are all equal in the eyes of the
> law. That's not the truth, because the eyes of the law are
> human eyes—yours and mine—and until we can see each
> other as equals, justice is never going to be evenhanded.
> It will remain nothing more than a reflection of our own
> prejudices. So, until that day, we have a duty under God to
> seek the truth, not with our eyes and not with our minds,
> where fear and hate turn commonality into prejudice, but
> with our hearts—where we don't know better.[2]

Until we can see each other as equals—as mothers and fathers, as sons and daughters—justice is never going to be evenhanded. Only when we share time together and *make it personal* will we lay aside the prejudice of our minds and experience the true understanding of our hearts. Only when we as blacks and whites watch our kids play together will we know that we all are created by God and are commonly human.

. . .

Kirsten and I now have four children. Two girls and two boys—Grace, Naomi, Judah, and Isaiah. As I write these words, we have one more child on the way.

> Only when we share time together and *make it personal* will we lay aside the prejudice of our minds and experience the true understanding of our hearts.

Something happens when we watch our kids play. Of course, there are sibling battles; jealousies; the inevitable tussles, squabbles, and fights; and the eventual tears. Sometimes it feels as if our kids will be the death of us.

But mostly they are the life of us.

We experience their exuberance at being able to run and jump, skip and leap. We experience their opening up to the world like little flowers. We experience their curiosity and fascination with learning about nature. We experience life in a new way through their lives.

Life. I am in favor of it. Yes, I am pro-life. And yes, I mean that in its usual sense—that the unborn fetus is a life to be protected. But I mean that in a different and larger way as well.

If we are in favor of the unborn life within, should we not also be in favor of the lives of people on the streets, in homes, in churches, and in our neighborhoods? In other neighborhoods? In the hood? If we are pro-life, should we not embrace young black lives as much as young white lives, and vice versa? If we are pro-life, should we not be about protecting life whether it is a fetus or a six-year-old or a teenager or a twentysomething young man on the street?

It is through those eyes that I see the lives of Michael Brown and Trayvon Martin and Eric Garner.

Being pro-life, I can't help but be *for* their lives and for the lives of others in similar circumstances. Because life is so precious to me, I feel deep sadness and anguish that these young men were killed.

In the aftermath of Trayvon Martin's death on the streets of Sanford, Florida, a movement called Black Lives Matter emerged. Through the tragedies of Michael Brown and Eric Garner, the movement gained momentum and is now a watchdog organization protesting a growing list of tragic injustices.

The lives of Michael Brown and Trayvon Martin and Eric Garner matter. Black lives matter. Our children's lives matter. *All* lives matter. And that's what being pro-life really means.

Being a parent, I feel all of this so deeply. I know, in watching my own children play, that they sometimes anger their brothers or sisters, sometimes steal or lie, and sometimes do wrong things. I am disappointed when I see them do these things; but because I also love them dearly, I try to pick them up out of their sin, set them back on a right path, and point them to a better choice next time.

> **Black lives matter. Our children's lives matter. *All* lives matter. And that's what being pro-life really means.**

Being my dad's son, I recall the time when he was so angry with me for that hip-hop tape and so disappointed in me for what I was listening to; and I recall other times, as well, when I chose badly, when I did wrong, when I sinned. But each time, my dad would pick me up out of my sin, set me back on a right path, and point me to a better choice next time.

Being a child of God, as I believe I am, I know that God is disappointed about those same wrong choices I've made. And yet amazingly, wondrously, incredibly, he is "pro-life," a cheerleader for *my* life; and he picks me up out of my sin, forgives me, and through the work of his Son gives me the righteousness that I do not deserve. That's a thing called grace.

. . .

I am sad for the parents of Michael and Trayvon and Eric and so many others.

I know that my own kids will someday be old enough to leave the house on their own for hours at a time. As much as I want to deny that day will come, it is inevitable. When that day comes, I will, like most parents, eagerly await their safe return.

How devastatingly horrible it must be for parents to be waiting for their son or daughter to return, only to get that dreaded phone call or foreboding knock at the door and be informed that their child is gone forever.

As a father, I hurt for those parents—of any race—whose children never came home. It is a blow to the gut that no parent should ever have to endure. And not only are parents and families mourning, but an entire community mourns as well.

It angers me to no end that, while people mourn, others have the nerve to insult them because they think the deceased somehow deserved this outcome. It infuriates me that some have the insensitivity to make comments about what kind of parent someone is. It's disgusting to see such insults hurled across social media.

I don't understand the argument from some that Michael Brown stole cigarillos from a store and that's why he was shot. I don't understand the claim that Eric Garner was selling cigarettes illegally and that's why he was choked to death. And I don't have the slightest idea why Trayvon Martin was confronted in the first place. Each one was the child of a parent. And as a parent, I can't help but think about my own kids leaving the house on some future day. Maybe one of them, God forbid, would do something wrong. I cannot imagine, and don't want to imagine, their lives being extinguished because of doing something wrong.

We all do wrong, the Bible says. Thank God that, by grace, we aren't killed because of it.

As we look at the stories and events and tragedies of racial conflict . . . no, let's make it more personal. As we look at people and lives and the victims of racial conflict, shouldn't we respond to them as a parent does—as God does—and be *for* the lives of Michael and Trayvon and Eric? And if they did wrong—if they stole something or sold something or did something—shouldn't we be disappointed by their choices and support legal consequences, yet strongly protest the events that got them killed?

If we are truly pro-life, shouldn't we be the first to express both grief and grace?

■ ■ ■

If you were on the jury in *A Time to Kill*, you would have heard Jake Brigance deliver his closing argument:

> Now I wanna tell you a story. I'm gonna ask y'all to close your eyes while I tell you this story. I want you to listen to me. I want you to listen to yourselves.
>
> This is a story about a little girl walking home from the grocery store one sunny afternoon. I want you to picture this little girl. Suddenly a truck races up. Two men jump out and grab her. They drag her into a nearby field and they tie her up, and they rip her clothes from her body. Now they climb on, first one, then the other, raping her, shattering everything innocent and pure in a vicious thrust,

in a fog of drunken breath and sweat. And when they're
done, after they've killed her tiny womb, murdered any
chance for her to bear children, to have life beyond her
own, they decide to use her for target practice. So they start
throwing full beer cans at her. They throw 'em so hard that
it tears the flesh all the way to her bones—and they urinate
on her.

Now comes the hanging. They have a rope; they tie a
noose. Imagine the noose pulling tight around her neck
and a sudden blinding jerk. She's pulled into the air and
her feet and legs go kicking and they don't find ground.
The hanging branch isn't strong enough. It snaps and
she falls back to the earth. So they pick her up, throw her
in the back of the truck, and drive out to Foggy Creek
Bridge and pitch her over the edge. And she drops some
thirty feet down to the creek bottom below. . . .

Can you see her? I want you to picture that little girl.
Now imagine she's white.[3]

With that, Brigance stops, letting the jury make it personal.

What if we were to consider the "other person" as one of our
own color, one of our own children? The tragedy of the racial
divide is that it simply isn't personal enough. For so many, it's
just an argument, a philosophy, a political position. A debate on
TV. But these people are not really human lives to us. Those lives
remain distant from us. And they are lives of a different color.

Now imagine it's your own child.

■ ■ ■

I'm a little further down the road of fatherhood than I was on
that 3 a.m. dash to the hospital with Kirsten in labor and a white

cop pulling us over. By now, Kirsten and I have a few years of experience as parents—learning about kids and watching them play—though just about every day is a new learning experience.

Sometimes we learn from our children about something inside ourselves.

Recently, Naomi came to me complaining that Grace, in an effort to skip the commercials on a movie they were watching together that we had recorded on TV, was purposely rewinding and fast-forwarding. There were certain commercials that Naomi wanted to watch, but her older sister, to demonstrate her control, knowingly sped through them, ignoring Naomi's request.

I went downstairs and explained to Grace how rude and inconsiderate that was. She apologized, and I placed the remote out of reach, forcing everyone to watch the commercials along with the movie. (What a novel idea!)

Ten minutes later, I heard Naomi pushing a large Tonka truck across the floor, its plastic wheels rattling loudly over the wood—quite a racket. Now it was Grace's turn to yell at Naomi for making it impossible to hear what was on TV.

I sat them down together and asked a simple question: How can you be upset with each other when you both do the same thing?

That's when the point of this gentle, teachable moment with my kids became a dagger in my own heart.

If we are serious about making the Michael Brown shooting personal, and if we are truly pro-life, shouldn't we consider the life of Darren Wilson as well?

■ ■ ■

I'm sympathetic because I wasn't there, so I don't know exactly what happened. Maybe Darren Wilson acted within his rights and duty as an officer of the law and killed Michael Brown in self-defense, like any of us would in the circumstance. Now he has to fear the backlash against himself and his loved ones when he was only doing his job. What a horrible thing to endure. Or maybe he provoked Michael and ignited the series of events that led to him eventually murdering the young man to prove a point.

This paragraph was hard for me to write in my Facebook post that night.

I believed—maybe because I had quickly jumped to "my side" of the issue—that Darren Wilson was a white cop who had acted out of a racial bias and deep prejudice and found (or created) a circumstance in which he could take out his racism by killing a young black man. The facts of the situation, we know now, are murky, and the steps taken in those moments cannot be verified one way or the other. And so you and I don't know what happened.

If we are serious about making the Michael Brown shooting personal, and if we are truly pro-life, shouldn't we consider the life of Darren Wilson as well?

Yes, I could replay the scene right now and walk us through it moment by moment. But that's not the point.

The point is that Darren Wilson has a life too. Somehow, if I am truly pro-life, I must be *for* Darren Wilson's life as much as I am *for* Michael Brown's life. This I must also make personal to myself.

But I confess I really don't want to.

. . .

For black people, forgiveness is a complex, messy, troubling thing.

As parents, we encounter the act of apology and forgiveness every day. A daughter complains, "You hurt me!" and a son eventually (with some urging) says, "I'm sorry." And then the daughter's slow reply, "That's okay." In another moment, they're playing together again. Apology and forgiveness, sweet and simple, a dozen times every day.

But we're not talking about fast-forwarding through TV commercials or the loud racket of a Tonka truck. We're talking about violence done to a son or daughter—sometimes brutal violence, sometimes killing. Sometimes someone is killed because of the color of his skin, because of an edge of racial hatred that a person brandishes in his heart, because of a seething rage that a person of one race fires at a person of another. Final moments of life and death are accompanied by a soundtrack—gruff voices of supremacy echoing the words and sins of centuries past.

I think some white people often don't understand that black forgiveness in these situations isn't about a careless accident. It's never easy to forgive someone who shot your son or daughter, of course, but it's a whole different reality when it seems clear that your child was killed for being black. A racial killing is violence against a race. As a black person myself, I see it as violence against me.

> For black people, forgiveness is a complex, messy, troubling thing. . . . We're talking about violence done to a son or daughter—sometimes brutal violence.

As survivors, friends, or family of a victim—or as members of a race that feels under attack—how can we forgive that?

Forgiveness isn't easy. And it shouldn't be.

German pastor Dietrich Bonhoeffer, who stood up against the prejudice and claims of Aryan supremacy of the Nazi regime during World War II (and who eventually gave his life in an effort to stop Hitler), also wrote and spoke against something he called *cheap grace*. He defined cheap grace as "the preaching of forgiveness without requiring repentance. . . . Cheap grace is grace without discipleship, grace without the cross, grace without Jesus Christ, living and incarnate."[4]

Forgiveness can be cheap as well—too cheap, too forced, too easy to mean anything. Yet it is pushed upon us. It is prompted by the news reporter with a microphone who asks the grieving mother, "Can you forgive?" long before she has had a chance to breathe, let alone mourn. It seems to be expected by white people—the wait-for-it moment of resolution at the end of the movie. I presume that this is because they don't know what else to say or do. Forced forgiveness is often the message of some churches and communities of faith, based on the assumption that this is what a good Christian is supposed to do. We want the feel-good ending. If only the survivor will say the right words, we think we can walk away feeling better about the world we have.

But there's nothing to feel good about. And cheap forgiveness is just empty words.

Black people struggle to forgive because white perpetrators struggle to repent. It's hard to forgive someone who hides behind the legal system, who can't or won't shed a tear for the life of someone's son or daughter or who points the finger at the victim. Repentance is a key requirement for forgiveness, according to the Bible.[5]

Yet we do forgive.

I think some black people instinctively understand that living in a constant state of unforgiveness is itself a kind of bondage. When we obsess over injustice and never let it go, it controls us, and we become slaves again. When Frederick Douglass, the slave-turned-reformer in the 1800s, famously forgave his former master, I think it was the final freedom for Douglass, the final step to becoming free from the hatred that had ruled his life.

During the writing of this book, another black life was tragically taken. Sam DuBose, a forty-three-year-old black man, was stopped by a white campus cop from the University of Cincinnati for the infraction of failing to display a front license plate. Before the traffic stop was over, DuBose had been shot in the head and killed.

At a press conference, DuBose's grieving mother, Audrey DuBose, quoted Psalm 93, which includes the verse, "The Lord on high is mightier than the noise of many waters, yea, than the mighty waves of the sea."[6] Later, speaking in church at her son's funeral, Audrey talked about Sam as her "complicated, challenging son."

"He loved life. He loved freedom. He was impossible," she said. The congregation, knowing the family, nodded and laughed. "But he brought me so much joy," Audrey said. "As much aggravation as he brought, he brought joy."

Audrey was asked by a reporter if she could "see in her heart" to forgive the cop who shot her son. She replied, "If he asks forgiveness, oh yeah, I can forgive him. I can forgive anybody; God forgave us. But . . . God . . . I . . . God already . . ."[7]

I think some black people instinctively understand that living in a constant state of unforgiveness is itself a kind of bondage.

I don't know what was going through Audrey's mind as she responded, but I think her answer—pauses, halting speech, and all—perfectly reflects the conflicted feelings that we as blacks feel.

Our theology says that forgiveness is based on repentance, yet no one has repented.

Our history reminds us that the violence we have experienced is hatred toward us as a different race.

Our instinct is to resent white people who want us to forgive too easily.

Our faith compels us to forgive anyway. Not in an easy way, but in a costly way. Not forgiveness that makes us feel better. Forgiveness that hurts but that ultimately sets us free.

That is the forgiveness of the gospel.

"Can you forgive?" is a trick question. If we say *yes*, it violates our true hearts and souls and walks us into cheap grace. If we say *no*, then we become the villains, the ones who seem difficult, cold, and lacking in compassion. Our best response is the one the world doesn't want to hear.

Our best response is just like Audrey DuBose's: filled with pauses, dotted with halting hesitations and silences, and stuffed with conflicted feelings and pain. And in our best response, we just might get to the other thing Audrey said: "I know the wrath of God. Also, I know the love of God."[8]

•   •   •

Lately, these issues of forgiveness, lives lost, and God's grace are all the more poignant. You see, Kirsten and I are expecting our fifth child, and our daughter will be born in just a few days.

I can't help but think that so much of the racial divide can be bridged in the presence of a newborn child. When that child is in the womb, we protect her life. When she is a newborn, we protect her life. When she is ten or twenty or thirty or beyond, we still, as parents, will protect her life in all kinds of ways. It doesn't matter if we are black or white—as parents, we do all we can to protect our children's lives.

And I think most of us want to prepare our children for this world we're in. We want to protect our children from the evils and injustice and dangers in culture and society. We can't, of course, not completely; but we still try. As I did a few days ago, in a letter to my unborn daughter.

My sweet baby girl,

We couldn't be more excited for your arrival. It's a trying time for all of us, as your birth is coming at one of the most hectic times of the year: NFL training camp. This is my twelfth season, and camp never gets any easier. In fact, it gets harder because I hate being away from your mom and your siblings for such a long time while I prepare for the upcoming football season. It's emotionally draining. As a dad, I sometimes feel helpless and guilty for leaving your mother all alone. One day you'll learn about Superwoman and realize she's your mom. You have siblings: four of them. Two older sisters and two older brothers. You, my dear, are in for a lifetime of adventure!

As I write this letter to you, I'm flying over Lake Pontchartrain, returning to West Virginia, where I've been in camp the last ten days. We had a day off, so I came down for twenty-four hours to see the family. I felt you kick a few times! I swear, when you hear my voice your activity skyrockets. Mommy says it feels like you are trying to get out, which you will be doing in a couple of weeks now. We all can't wait to meet you, and the plan is for my hands to be the first hands you meet. As soon as I get word, I'm coming home from camp—catching you is way more important than catching a football.

There's so much for you to know and learn about the world you are coming into. As I fly over it now, it looks so peaceful and beautiful. God's creation is awe inspiring, a living testament to his existence. I can't wait to take you to the beaches and mountains, to show you butterflies and lizards, and to comfort you during your first thunderstorm.

While the world we have is one of wondrous beauty, it is also one of pain, anguish, guilt, failure, and hate. Some people will not like you because of your skin tone. They will speak ill of you without even knowing you, assuming the worst. Their words and deeds may demean you and others who look like you, even though, as your sister Grace prays at night, "No one should treat anyone different because of their skin tone, because God made us that way and gave us different talents." As you grow older, you will learn about our history, black people's history, in America. It has been a path filled with tears and triumph, pain and pride, survival and success.

No doubt you will hear about great women such as Harriet Tubman and Sojourner Truth, who helped free people from bondage. You will know about leaders like Martin Luther King Jr., Frederick Douglass, and W. E. B. Du Bois. In school you will learn about Madam C. J. Walker, a successful black entrepreneur; inventor Lewis Latimer, who helped to patent the original telephone and the electric light bulb; and Mae Jemison, the first black woman to travel into space. I say that no doubt you will hear about these great people, but the truth is I can only hope *that you will. Honestly, you may wonder why we learn so little about our black history in school. It may leave you to wonder how much we really matter.*

But while we celebrate these icons of our legacy, the overwhelming impression of your skin will be negative, a lingering and infectious effect of our beginnings on this continent. Blackness will be cast as a shadow of inferiority. If you're like me, when you see it on the news or hear it in everyday conversation, you'll hate it. Your once "so cute" brothers will one day be strong black men, who could be considered "threatening." You and your sisters will be smart and beautiful and charismatic like your mom. Because of that, you'll be accepted by many white people as an "exception" among your race, yet despised by many blacks as "Boojie" as if you've forgotten who you are, where you came from, or who you should be. Things here are so sadly twisted.

My sweet baby girl, because sin entered the world, the beautiful peace I witness from my airplane window right now was traded for the hatred, fear, frustration, prejudice, and lawlessness we experience below the clouds. So when you hear that first N-word, and when you realize you are different, I want you to remember that your heart needs redemption just as much as the ones who mistreat you. I want you to stand for justice for all people, speaking the truth in love, never condoning wrongdoing but instead forgiving, because forgiveness sets the forgiver free from the consuming fire of vengeance. I want you to approach people as individuals, understanding that not all whites are against you and that not all blacks have your best interests at heart. I want you to defy the limits and expectations others may have for you, realizing that your opportunities are exponentially greater than for those who came before you. I want you to love people with the love of Christ, not seeing the outward appearance but looking at what's under their skin, in their hearts.

You come from a rich heritage of godly men and women who have blazed a trail before you. They have come to understand that it's not about them but about God. They've experienced the worst of the racial divide and bias in America, yet they have accomplished great things in education, business, ministry, and family, becoming bridges for others to unite regardless of the shade of their skin. This wasn't easy. The easy thing to do is to remain angry. And don't get me wrong—there is a time for that. Sometimes there is a need for that. But I have a greater hope for your generation. That you are willing to honestly look within yourself and confront these ills, leading to a revival of changed hearts. As deep as the divide is now, always remember that it's not in our own power, but in the power of God, that this change will happen.

The day is drawing near. You will be in my arms soon.

I already love you,

Daddy

7

OFFENDED

I'M OFFENDED
because of the insulting comments I've seen
that are not only insensitive but dismissive
to the painful experiences of others.

EVEN THOUGH THE SPORTS WORLD is filled with accomplished black players, it's not uncommon for black people to be called niggers—in the stands, where we can't hear it, or a little closer, where we can. Often it's just bizarre: In one moment we are held high as heroes, asked for autographs, and begged to kiss babies; in the next moment, in the aftermath of a bad play, we are called one of the most offensive terms in the English language.

University of Michigan quarterback Devin Gardner has experienced this more times than he can count. In the aftermath of a difficult year, he estimates he's seen more than one thousand negative comments toward him on Twitter. "I've been called the N-word so many times this year," Gardner said. "One guy told me I was the N-word, and said I know N-words can't play quarterback. And I was like, are we not past this? Say what you want about my skill, but come on."[1]

For black players, name-calling is something we've come to accept as part of the game, yet the N-word in particular is pointedly demeaning. When we're on the field, we can't help but notice that almost everyone in the stadium is white. So what is this about? Are the black players simply seen as we were in the circuses of old—as entertainment for white people? Rather than throw baseballs at the face of a black person in the "game" of African Dodger, do people today launch the N-word at us instead?

I don't want to say that in professional sports we black players get used to being called hateful things, because it always digs deep. It's not something we should ever get used to. But we do get to a point where, sadly, we expect it. Sure, I know the passion and futility that sports fans express, and yelling and shouting are part of the experience of sports fan-dom. But do people not know what the N-word means? Do they not know how it refers to someone being less than human? Do they not understand how it recalls and justifies slavery? In using the N-word, are people just ignorant, or are they racist? Probably both.

For black players, name-calling is something we've come to accept as part of the game, yet the N-word in particular is pointedly demeaning.

During training camp, we practice at a facility that's a two-minute ride from our dorm rooms. The team hires shuttles, luxury Mercedes, and GMC SUVs to take us back and forth throughout the day. The drivers are young college guys, most of them white and many with some relationship to the front office. They are good kids, and I've enjoyed small talk with some of them on these short rides.

But it's always interesting to get into the car and hear their choice of music. Usually it's some form of hip-hop. I'm not sure if that's what they think *we* want to hear, or if it's what they were already listening to. I think it's the latter—they usually recite the words along with the radio.

What's interesting is that, when they recite the words to the songs when black players are in the car, they carefully omit the N-word when it pops up in the lyrics. And that's usually quite often.

I feel uncomfortable at these times. First, because we are in what black people call *mixed company*, I always wonder what they are thinking. I'm not naive enough to assume they don't recite the songs word-for-word when blacks aren't present, and honestly,

I'm not mad at them for it. But I know there is an uneasiness when blacks are around because of everything implied by that word.

The point is, they know the word is offensive. They are not ignorant of its meaning or its effect. To their credit, they are sensitive enough not to say those words in front of us. To their shame, they still play songs that use the N-word.

Many times, I request that they change the station or at least turn it down when I'm in the passenger seat. I don't want them to conclude that I, a black man, am in agreement with the use of the N-word in music or conversation, thus empowering them to feel free to use it too. If I don't say anything, who will?

But this goes to the point that many often bring up—that blacks use the N-word among themselves in the context of black culture and music. The argument typically goes that black people have some *right* to use the word among themselves, whereas white people don't have that right, and that therefore, by using the word themselves, black people to some degree defang the term and make it somehow less repulsive and hateful.

The argument typically goes that black people have some *right* to use the N-word among themselves, whereas white people don't have that right.

Recently, in a conversation with a Jewish teammate, I asked him his thoughts about the use of the N-word by and among black people. He said he thought we did it to "embrace and neutralize the word. To turn something that was bad into something positive." I then asked him if he and his family ever used certain Jewish slurs—and I named a couple of words that I'd heard and considered reprehensible. Did Jews use those words among themselves to diminish their power?

"No," he said.

I suspect that this points in some way to the complete reassignment of identity unique to the experience of African descendants on a new continent, in a new culture, and in a new state of being—a slate that was purposely wiped clean and reassigned. The mental ripples of those days are what we all, white and black, continue to subconsciously live out today.

So yes, I understand some of the cultural and social reasons black people might use the N-word.

But I don't buy it.

The N-word is a hateful word, no matter who uses it. It's the trademark of white supremacist terrorism. It is the keyword of the sorry legacy of slavery. It is the symbol of inhumanity. It's often the flashpoint of racial conflict and violence. I don't see how it is constructive, edifying, or proper for anyone of any race to use it.

Even as I proclaim that view with deep conviction, I confess that I'm also talking to myself. I, too, have been caught up in the aspects of black culture that justify the use of the N-word apart from its use in white culture. I, too, have used the N-word to describe others. And though I try to keep my home and family "N-word free," I know I've been guilty. Guilty as sin.

■ ■ ■

When we think of things that are racially offensive, we start with the N-word. But as we all know, it goes far beyond that today.

We've all heard the hate of anonymous voices. We know about the dark corners of the Internet, such as some of the group chatter on Reddit, in which hate speech of all kinds—toward blacks and women in particular—is given free rein. We know about the secret societies that still advocate white supremacy. We've read the vile manifesto of the Charleston shooter, Dylann

Roof. We may remember the disgusting comments that people posted in response to the CNN video interview with the mothers of Michael and Trayvon and Eric. The list goes on and on.

It's too easy to point our fingers at all of this and condemn others for their offending beliefs, actions, and words. But the real problem of racial offense in the world is not in the use of the N-word. It's not in the anonymous trolling on the Internet, or in the hateful thoughts of white kids who grow up to be terrorists. It's not in the social cracks and crevices where the extremists reside.

> **The real problem of racial offense is in the living rooms, classrooms, workplaces, and stadiums of America, where we make casual and ignorant assumptions about race.**

The real problem of racial offense is in the living rooms, classrooms, workplaces, and stadiums of America, where the rest of us make casual and ignorant assumptions about race.

The real problem of offense is not *out there* in others. It's inside our own hearts and minds.

■　■　■

Growing up, I went to a school that was mostly white. It wasn't long before I figured out that I was *supposed* to be good at sports. I felt that assumption whenever white people looked at me. Of course, I happened to be athletic and had the physique, but clearly there was something beyond that in what people said and how they looked at me. I was black, and therefore it was assumed I would excel in sports.

The black kid was always supposed to be able to run fast and jump high. At field day, if I didn't win the races, it was, well, surprising (and disappointing). Truth be told, I didn't dominate everything; there were other kids—white kids—in my classes who were as talented as I was. But the expectation was that I would always do well as an athlete. Because I was black.

Coming out of high school, I first went to Duke before transferring to the University of Georgia, where I finished my college education and my college football career. I remember facing the stereotype in college that I was only there for my athletic talent. Conversations often revealed an assumption that I must have gotten in on an athletic scholarship. Of course, the unspoken subtext was, *It couldn't possibly have been an academic scholarship, because he's black.*

On more than one occasion, I had to put a fellow student in his place, comparing SAT scores to prove I "deserved" to be there, as well as explaining the financial contribution my athletic participation made to the institution. (Of course, I quickly learned that I couldn't continue to do that—it simply made me the "mean black guy" or the black man with an attitude.)

I saw black students steered toward "athlete-friendly" majors. It seemed the bar was set low for many of my black teammates. They were encouraged to declare majors that would limit their career paths, while our white teammates were involved in educational programs that would give them more effective career paths after football. What disturbed me the most was that it was the guidance counselors, whether intentionally or not, who directed these athletes in this manner. The combination of coaches wanting to keep athletes eligible, counselors feeling pressure and dealing with their own biases, and athletes entering college with varying levels of preparedness led to black athletes being exploited. I remember speaking with teammates about this, persuading them to take "harder" majors that their counselors or coaches, and maybe even they themselves, doubted that they could complete.

It's offensive when someone looks at me and says something that assumes that, because I'm black, I must be athletic and not quite up to par intellectually. And yet that happens all the time.

Recently, I spoke at a church in Buckhead, in Atlanta. Afterward, a white man whom I quickly recognized as a college friend from my days at Georgia came up to me. After we reminisced for a while, he surprised me by apologizing.

"Benjamin," he said, "after all these years, I've been troubled about something I said to you back then."

I looked at him, puzzled. I didn't recall anything he'd said or done to offend me.

He recounted a question he had asked me when we were both part of a leadership program for student athletes at Georgia: "How'd you get into this program?" He said that my immediate reaction had troubled him. "Benjamin, you looked at me so upset. And that has always stuck in my head."

Frankly, I didn't recall the conversation, though I realized that my reaction must have been intense enough to cause him to remember it. And I could imagine myself responding that way. It rang true.

He went on to say that, over the years, he'd grown a lot, read things about race, and recently followed some of my writings online. And he realized later how I must have taken his simple comment that day.

"Benjamin, I'm sorry. I've been waiting for a chance to apologize to you. I never meant to offend you. I wasn't suggesting by what I said that you didn't *deserve* to be in the program. I was just asking about what made you sign up for it, why that interested you, and how that interest drew you to the program."

In that moment, I was pointed to my own internal sensitivity. I was so primed to assume that a white guy in college would doubt my intelligence just because I was black that that was what I heard, even though it wasn't what he had intended.

I apologized to him. "I just assumed you were talking bad about black people, talking bad about me as a black athlete. That's not what you were doing. I'm sorry for being so defensive."

I was so primed to assume that a white guy in college would doubt my intelligence just because I was black that that was what I heard.

"In light of everything I've learned in the last ten years," he replied, "I understand how what I said got under your skin. That's why I wanted to talk with you."

In the days since that encounter, I've thought about what happened. In one sense, it was a microcosm of how the racial divide develops and widens. How a simple remark offends us, even though it might not have been intended that way, and how the offense can settle in and becomes a breach in a relationship—and in a society.

In another sense, it's an example of how two people, white and black, can address what offends, what is assumed, what is judged, and what can be made right.

What if more white people would come forward and say, "I didn't mean to suggest . . ."?

What if more black people could overcome their sensitivity and confess, "I'm sorry. I shouldn't have taken it that way . . ."?

∎ ∎ ∎

I remember when the word *wigger* became popular.

I was in grade school. I cringed whenever I heard classmates tell each other they were acting like wiggers. Already knowing the answer, I would ask them what it meant.

"Uh, well, it's a white person who acts black," they'd reply.

I remember assuming my best lawyer impersonation and asking them as if they were on the witness stand: "If a wigger is a white person who acts black, what is a black person called?"

Immediately understanding my line of reasoning, they back-pedaled faster than Deion Sanders, claiming, "I didn't mean that." I never believed them, thinking that no one could be that naive and ignorant. But maybe, just maybe, I was too harsh. Can you say things like that and just be thoughtless? Perhaps.

I have a white friend, one of my teammates on the New Orleans Saints, with whom I talk about all kinds of things, frequently including race issues. He shared with me a story about the word *wigger*.

Now in his tenth year in the NFL, he recalled a time early in his career when he uncharacteristically and ignorantly used *wigger* in a conversation with a mixed group of guys, white and black. Now able to laugh about it, he described the abrupt and uncomfortable silence that followed, accompanied by stares of disbelief from the other players.

Fortunately for him, before everyone could jump down his throat, a close friend who was black pulled him aside and gave him a chance to explain what in the world he was thinking.

Although he'd always known in a general sense what it meant, he had never taken the logical steps to consider the origins of the word and why it might be considered offensive. He said it was just a word he'd heard at times and in his ignorance had carelessly adopted. He had not intended to be malicious or offensive. Yet whatever his intentions, he acknowledged that his use of the word was offensive to black people.

I think his story illustrates an important point. So-called *good* people may think they aren't insulting to black people, and they may not intend to be; yet they can readily say things that are offensive. And to a great degree, it's because we harbor two separate compartments inside ourselves: one that holds on to these words, biases, and prejudices that we keep for private use when among those of our own race; and another for when we're in mixed company.

So-called *good* people may think they aren't insulting to black people, and they may not intend to be; yet they can readily say things that are offensive.

Some would say the problem is that the prejudice of one compartment leaks into the other compartment. I believe the problem is that we have a racist compartment inside us in the first place. The problem isn't how we appear to others. It's what's inside us, what's in our hearts and minds. That's who we are.

This same white teammate recently became an uncle. His sister had a baby girl—by a black man. And now my friend's perspective has changed completely. He's now utterly aware of the landscape of racial words and slurs that swirl around conversations everywhere. He sees the racial environment in terms of how they might hurt the little niece he loves so dearly.

It's another one of those "imagine she's white" or "imagine she's black" moments. If it is someone close to you—your daughter or niece, son or nephew—how would the words you speak be felt by him or her?

All of these events have brought my friend and me closer together. Our conversations have gotten a bit deeper. Recently, we discussed the implications of Rachel Dolezal's deception (the white woman who posed as black and became an NAACP chapter leader in the state of Washington) and black America's vehement reaction. Earlier, when I had written the Facebook post about Ferguson, my friend was one of the first teammates to tell me how much he appreciated my words. He continued to comment about every media and talk show appearance I made, as well, joking that I was going to run for president.

Not likely. I like to speak my mind too much!

. . .

Our words are not the only way that we offend one another. Our symbols also have the power to affront.

When I was growing up, my family moved to South Carolina. In high school there, one of my closest friends was a football player named Frank.

Frank was about five-eleven and 185 pounds, but somehow he played offensive guard—and survived! He was scrappy and always held his own.

Frank was also white. Very white. Literally: He had really, really pale skin. He was also very funny. Frank was one of the fastest runners the track team had. In the spring, when track was in full gear, Frank would always boast about how he was going to get a great tan that year. And the day after every track meet, without exception, he would walk into class vividly, radiantly, crisply sunburned.

During our high school years, Frank and I became pretty close friends, spending time at each other's homes on a regular basis. I remember the first time I visited his house. His parents were two of the most gracious people I had ever met, and I immediately felt like one of the family. Frank gave me the house tour, ending at his own bedroom. When he opened the door and I walked in, I was ill prepared for what I saw.

Hanging above his bed was a large Confederate flag.

The sight of the "Southern Cross" had become quite familiar since my family's move to South Carolina. It seemed to be embedded in the culture. Bumper stickers, license plates, and T-shirts all proudly displayed the banner, signifying its prominent place in Southern culture. In fact, the flag flew atop the statehouse in Columbia, suggesting a state government that favored slavery, segregation, and the suppression of black people. For me, the flag was a reminder of the pain, terrorism, oppression, and death inflicted on thousands of blacks.

In mid-November of 2001, during my second year at the University of Georgia, the Bulldogs traveled to Oxford, Mississippi, to play Ole Miss. I had never been to the state or the school before. I was a little nervous about the game. Not long after we took the field for pregame warm-ups, I heard the tune "Dixie" in the air. I turned to see Colonel Reb and the Ole Miss band marching into Vaught-Hemingway Stadium. I stared for a moment in disbelief, but it clearly wasn't a joke.

The sight of the "Southern Cross" had become quite familiar since my family's move to South Carolina. It seemed to be embedded in the culture.

Unbelievably, this was their school song! Did they not know that "Dixie" was made popular through the blackface minstrelsy of the nineteenth century? Those minstrel shows lampooned black people as dim-witted, lazy, buffoonish, superstitious, happy-go-lucky, and musical. Yet this signature song was what the band played as they marched onto the field for a college football game, represented by a team full of black student athletes.

Maybe I overreacted. I've had this discussion with white friends and black friends who attended Ole Miss. Though they tell me the school has race issues like any other institution, they also assure me that Ole Miss is not a racist school. Nevertheless, that *was* my reaction. I remember, throughout the game, getting in my stance and looking at the brown face across from me, wondering if it bothered him as much as it bothered me.

In the wake of the Charleston shooting, which prompted the controversy surrounding the Confederate flag at the South Carolina statehouse, I wrote a Facebook post expressing how I felt.

The Rebel Flag

It's hard to explain how I feel when I see the rebel flag. The emotional bucket overflows with anger, trepidation, sorrow, a perverted pride and apathy. As hard as I try not to make assumptions about whoever is flying the flag or driving around with it mounted on their truck, my mind cannot hold back the painful images of the past generations . . . and the current one. The nine racially motivated murders of last week have written a new chapter in the annals of race violence in this country. And at the center of it all, proudly displayed in images of the killer, the rebel flag.

When I moved to South Carolina in 1996, albeit from the southern state of Virginia, I was somewhat taken aback by the frequency of which I saw the flag. It was on vehicles, displayed on homes, and worn on T-shirts. Like grits and sweet tea, the flag was just part of the culture, an enduring symbol of all things Southern. This never changed how I felt about it, but it did teach me to give individuals a certain amount of grace and realize that not everyone who embraced the flag embraced prejudice and supremacy alike.

I can remember visiting a teammate's home for the first time [during] my sophomore year. Frank, a white offensive guard on my high school football team, had quickly become my closest friend, welcoming me, the new guy, when others weren't so quick to do so. As I walked into his room, I froze, staring uncomfortably at the large Rebel flag hanging above his bed. I remember the lump in my throat as I briefly attempted to convey, in the most non-condemning way, what the flag represented to me and many others like me. Because of the lingering heaviness of the moment, I can't recall much after that, but I do remember how valued I felt when I returned to Frank's home some time later and the flag was gone! He didn't have to, but because he cared about our friendship, because he cared about me, he empathetically removed the offensive banner on my behalf and maybe for the first time heard how painful that symbol could be. That day was a turning point in our relationship, and today Frank continues to be one of my best friends.

It should not take the brutal, senseless killings of innocent black Americans in a church by a young white man to ensure the removal of the Confederate battle flag from the statehouse grounds where it has flown in proud defiance of the civil rights movement since the 1960s. If the flag wasn't problematic before this heinous crime, it should not be problematic now; and to hastily remove it in response to this slaughter, although a sympathetic (and economic) gesture, does not address the heart of the matter. In my estimation, it is indeed the HEART that is the matter. Displaying the Confederate flag is not inherently wrong. This is not NECESSARILY an issue on which we can take a moral stance. It is not a simple right or wrong dilemma. I understand that for some the Confederate battle flag does not evoke sentiments of racism or supremacy; it is simply a tribute to their heritage, ancestors, and homeland. For others, including the killer, it means much more, and for others it is a hiding place for passive racism and group "identity." It is without a doubt, however, a litmus test, exposing our willingness to deny our liberty, our freedom, to fly the flag of our choice, for the sake of offending our countrymen whose SHARED HERITAGE is conversely stained with death, injustice, rape, terror, and inferiority.

If we remove the Confederate flag from the state capitol for any reason other than a change in the hearts of South

*Carolinians, we may as well leave it be. This is not the
time for political statements and worrying about national
perception. But if we, like my friend Frank, finally listen to
the cries and concerns of those we say we care about, soften
our hearts, and choose to lay our liberties aside to assuage
the pain of our brothers, the only suitable option would be
a unanimous decision to remove the flag from the public
grounds at the Palmetto State capitol. The past and its people,
as acclaimed or afflicted as they may be, should always be
remembered. But it is difficult to completely "move forward"
if painful, divisive icons continue to stand unchallenged.*

*Sometimes, tragedies have a way of jolting us, laying the
truth about us, individually and collectively, stark naked for
all to see. The outpouring for Charleston has been nothing
short of extraordinary and inspiring. Sometimes it takes one
person, one neighborhood, one city, and one state to show the
unifying love of Christ to the world. As a canyon is carved by
the flow of a river long dried up, may the passion of this week
cut deep, leaving a permanent change in hearts and souls long
after the emotion has gone.*

■ ■ ■

This isn't about political correctness or making a list of forbidden
words and symbols that we must constantly update and commit
to memory to avoid using the wrong way or in the wrong situations in mixed company. This isn't about constantly worrying
that we're saying the wrong thing to the wrong person at the
wrong time.

It isn't that complicated. Yet in many ways, it's even more difficult because it's about how we view other people and how we
understand their stories.

Recently, a TED Talk video by a black novelist and speaker named Chimamanda Ngozi Adichie went viral. In a brief nineteen minutes, Adichie gets to the heart of racism and offense.[2]

Her message in "The Danger of a Single Story" is simple: Each of us is composed of multiple overlapping stories. I am, for example, a football player, a father, a son, a husband, a college graduate with a degree in finance, a Christian, and a black man. Yet if you see me, talk to me, or talk about me based on just one of the many stories that make up who I am, you reduce me to a single story.

If you see me, talk to me, or talk about me based on just one of the many stories that make up who I am, you reduce me to a single story.

Adichie speaks about her family in Nigeria. Both her parents were accomplished professionals, and they hired domestics to help them maintain their home. Adichie learned to read when she was four, and she read books from around the world while growing up.

She tells about her arrival at an American university. Her new American roommate didn't know what to make of her. When the roommate asked how Adichie had learned to speak such good English, Adichie calmly informed her that English was the official language of Nigeria. The roommate, now very confused, asked to listen to Adichie's "tribal music." Adichie pulled out her tape of Mariah Carey. The roommate later assumed that Adichie didn't know how to operate a stove. Over and over, she misjudged Adichie based on a single assumed story.

Adichie goes on:

What struck me was this—she had felt sorry for me even before she saw me. Her default position toward me as an African was a kind of patronizing, well-meaning pity. My roommate had a single story of Africa, a single story of catastrophe. In this single story, there was no possibility of Africans being similar to her in any way, no possibility of feelings more complex than pity, no possibility of a connection as human equals.[3]

Later in her TED Talk, Adichie points the finger at herself, telling of a trip to Mexico and of her assumptions about Mexicans as people given to fleecing the health care system, sneaking across the border, and being arrested. But then she spent some time in Mexico—seeing people going to work, shopping in the marketplace, and laughing—and she caught herself in a moment of shame. She knew she had bought into a single story about an entire nation of people.

Adichie says, "That is how to create a single story. Show a people as one thing, as only one thing, over and over again, and that is what they become."[4]

The consequence of the single story is this: It robs people of dignity. It makes our recognition of our equal humanity difficult. It emphasizes how we are different, rather than how we are similar. It reduces people to just one thing, based on a stereotype.

That's the thing about racial offensiveness. It isn't only the crass comments that matter; it's the feeling and meaning behind the words that fail to or refuse to see people, white or black, as the complex human beings they are. Racial slurs are a way of diminishing a person to a single thing, a lesser thing, a less-than-human thing.

When we reduce someone else's humanity to a single story, we can for a moment feel superior. And this is actually the appeal of racism. It's a reduction of a race of people to a stereotype. That reduction makes some people feel more powerful, even though they aren't. Racism is inherently immature, a form of cowardice, often hiding anonymously within a group that chatters the same things.

Even so, racial offensiveness has its impact. We react, we internalize the hate, and we start to make up our own single story about the other person. A cycle continues.

Racism is inherently immature, a form of cowardice, often hiding anonymously within a group that chatters the same things.

Yes, I am offended by the insulting things that people say and do, by the symbols they embrace, and by the single story they perpetuate. Quite frankly, I think that a lot of this emerges from sin in our hearts that we need to repent of.

And I think the rest of it is just pure evil.

I believe evil exists because I believe Satan exists. The enemy of our souls really doesn't care what clothes his evil wears. In some cases, his evil is achieved through the drug culture. In other cases, his evil is accomplished through sex slavery. In many cases, his evil is manifested through racial hate, hate speech, and white supremacy. And he uses the racial sins of all of us to fuel it.

I don't know how we can look at the legacy of racial injustice in our country and be blind to its origins. How can we see the history of slavery, of Jim Crow, and of the violence of modern-day racial conflict and not see the supernatural forces that conspire to perpetuate it? How can we look at the Charleston shootings and not understand them as what they clearly are—despicable, horrifying evil?

Yes, evil exists. And it often wears the cloak of racism.

HOPELESS

I'M HOPELESS
because I've lived long enough to expect things like
this to continue to happen. I'm not surprised, and at
some point my little children are going to inherit the
weight of being a minority and all that it entails.

GRANDDADDY HAD BIG HANDS. He used to box when he was a young man. Supposedly, he was pretty good in the ring and was asked to turn pro and move to New York. But he was in love with a girl named Dicey and didn't want to leave her.

Granddaddy married Dicey and they settled in the Norfolk area, in an all-black apartment community called Marshall Manor, an affordable-income development just outside of downtown.

In the late '60s, they moved across the Campostella Bridge to a white neighborhood called Campostella Heights. It was where my dad grew up. It was where I grew up.

Once Granddaddy got himself married, he had to set aside boxing and take a job. Actually, two jobs. He worked at the Naval Operating Base, which back then was significant employment for a black man. He directed planes onto the base and loaded and unloaded the freight. He also took on a night job at the officer's club. He'd work until 4:30 p.m. at the naval station, come home, have dinner, and then go to the officer's club at about 10:30.

I wouldn't say he was a warm and fuzzy kind of granddad. Quiet and emotionally closed by nature, he was nonetheless responsible and dedicated—a family man. He knew that it was important for a man to work hard to provide. With my grandma working as a domestic, they made a decent life together.

They took pride in owning a home, and I remember Granddaddy always having a meticulous yard. He kept the lawn neatly mowed and the bushes and hedges perfectly trimmed. His edging was the best I've ever seen. He didn't use a weed whacker; he did the work manually, using a flat hoe. This made lines so deep between the grass and the sidewalk that you could sprain an ankle if you weren't careful.

Granddaddy was always good to me. Whenever I walked over to their house, I would find him tinkering with his cars. He loved cars, loved fixing them up, loved having nice vehicles in the driveway. He didn't talk a lot, but I enjoyed hanging out with him.

His big hands, no longer used for boxing, had another purpose: cutting my hair. I remember his hands holding my head still while he clipped, his thumb on my forehead just above my eye socket, and his large palm tilting my head when he needed to trim the sides.

Granddaddy had a nickname: Watusi. I know it's an African tribe and also the name of a '60s dance craze, but to this day I don't know why it was Granddaddy's nickname. I've kind of adopted the idea that he was at one time a pretty good dancer. In any case, he loved his nickname and wore it proudly. One of his cars bore a WATUSI 1 license plate. The other car's license plate read WATUSI 2.

Because Granddaddy had been a boxer, he was a big fan of it on TV. Those were the days of Lennox Lewis and Mike Tyson and the later career of George Foreman. Granddaddy got HBO so he could watch the fights, and I remember going over there sometimes to watch with him.

I remember, too, how my dad and granddaddy and I would talk about football. My dad had played at the University of Maryland, and I was playing in high school, so football was in our blood.

Daddy and I would toss the football around in our backyard all the time. But there's one special time with my grandfather that I remember warmly. It was during the years when my family was living in South Carolina and I came back to Norfolk for a visit. I remember going over to Granddaddy's house and finding him in the backyard. Granddaddy dug out an old fielder's mitt and handed it to me. It was one of the ancient kind—a flat, old baseball glove of worn leather. We played catch, just the two of us.

I don't know why that sticks with me. Maybe because it was a time when I was most impressionable as a kid, and playing sports with my granddad stamped a vivid memory in my mind right then. Maybe it was the feeling of having my granddaddy include me in his life by handing me his old, worn baseball leather. Or maybe it was some sense I had—even then, early in my life—that there weren't really enough hopeful moments in the lives of black families, even ours; and yet in a simple game of catch, there was a promise of how the world could be.

Whatever the reason, the image of that time is indelible. I can still recall those moments: the sound of the ball smacking into my glove and the feeling of winding up and firing the ball back like I was Roger Clemens. I don't know why, but when I think of Granddaddy now, I think of that day: a perfect afternoon when everything was right, and the lazy, easy rhythm of playing catch.

■ ■ ■

When Granddaddy took Dicey over the bridge into Campostella Heights, he crossed a bridge in time, as well. He had grown up in an America that treated black people as second-class citizens and inferior human beings. He moved into an America where black people dared to live beside whites as equals.

Toward the end of World War II, the naval base at Norfolk

became the intake point for Nazi German prisoners. Granddaddy, in his work there loading and unloading planes, would be near the place where the prisoners were kept. The only thing was, if he needed to use the bathroom, he wasn't allowed to use the one that the prisoners and the white workers could use. He had to walk clear around the base to the "colored" bathroom. The white Nazis had more privilege than a black American.

When my dad was growing up, my granddaddy would tell him how it used to be—how when he passed a white woman on the street, he was to look down and never look her in the eye.

He had grown up in an America that treated black people as second-class citizens and inferior human beings.

"No way," my dad would say.

"That's the way it was," my granddaddy would say. And back then my grandmother, while shopping in clothing stores, was required to put a plastic bag on her head before trying on hats.

That was the America that Granddaddy moved out of when he crossed the Campostella Bridge. He not only stepped into the white neighborhood of Campostella Heights, but at the same time, he walked into the 1960s.

Later, in 1963, President John F. Kennedy, a man widely embraced as "the friend of black people everywhere," was killed.

The '60s were also a time of white flight, when white people began to move out of neighborhoods that black people moved into.

It was a time of forced integration of black kids into white schools. As part of the busing program, Granddaddy and Grandma would eventually send my dad across town to a new high school.

In 1968, Martin Luther King Jr. was shot and killed in Memphis. Riots broke out in sixty American cities following his assassination. But one city in particular—Indianapolis—experienced no rioting. This was attributed to a speech made by one of the candidates then running for president. The speech was delivered in a downtown Indianapolis ghetto and called for black people "to tame the savageness of man and make gentle the life of this world."[1] Indianapolis listened, and peace reigned.

Two months later, the man who had delivered that speech— Robert Kennedy—was shot to death at a Los Angeles hotel during a campaign stop.

So long ago, and yet not so long ago.

. . .

My Facebook post in response to the Ferguson grand jury decision was posted on November 25, 2014. During the nine months before my post and the nine months afterward, here are some of the events that took place:

- July 17, 2014: Eric Garner was killed while being arrested in Staten Island, New York.
- August 9, 2014: Michael Brown was shot and killed by police officer Darren Wilson in Ferguson, Missouri.
- November 24, 2014: Protesters in Ferguson, on hearing of the grand jury's decision not to indict Darren Wilson, rioted violently in the streets.
- April 4, 2015: Walter Scott was shot dead by a police officer in North Charleston, South Carolina.
- June 17, 2015: Nine black people were killed by a white supremacist at Emanuel African Methodist Episcopal Church in Charleston, South Carolina.
- August 9, 2015: People in Ferguson rioted and looted following a peaceful demonstration commemorating the anniversary of Michael Brown's death.

This covers just over a year, and it isn't even everything—not even close.

My dad, remembering those years growing up in Campostella Heights on the other side of the bridge and the killings and riots of that decade, said in response to these recent events, "It's as bad as I've seen it since the '60s."

I think about this history—*our* history; about my granddaddy moving into a white neighborhood and his world during the civil rights '60s; about my dad as a kid in Campostella Heights, bullied for being black and subjected to the necessary evil of busing; and about my own life there, in the same neighborhood growing up. Three generations. Has anything changed? Has anything gotten better?

I think about this history—*our* history. . . . Three generations. Has anything changed? Has anything gotten better?

I can see that, yes, some things have changed. Black people have, I believe, more opportunity than in my granddaddy's day. Black people have access to better education overall than in my father's school-age years. Yet black men still make less money for the same jobs as white men, education is still unequal, and we are still largely a segregated society, each race continuing to head for its respective corner.

Today, just as it was fifty years ago—in almost a mirror image of the 1960s—rioting has erupted out of discontentment, anger, and outrage. Bias and prejudice are nurtured and hidden in the strongholds of authority, much as they were in the time of George Wallace. And people are getting killed. Today, it's not our leaders and presidents who are killed. Today, it's our kids. On the streets. Or in a church Bible study.

So, forgive me for feeling hopeless.

∎ ∎ ∎

For the sake of our kids, we search desperately for a more positive future.

Certainly the younger generation, millennials, are less prejudiced than their parents—you would think. But as the *Washington Post* reports, citing research from the General Social Survey, millennials are just as likely to harbor racial biases as their baby-boomer parents.[2]

Certainly there are fewer white supremacy groups in America today than there were ten years ago—you would think. But no, hate groups are not only multiplying in number but also increasing in size. One online white supremacy hate group has increased its membership by 50 percent over the past five years.[3]

Certainly the election of America's first black president would usher in a new era of black-white understanding—you would think. But no, according to a 2012 AP poll, 51 percent of Americans now express "anti-black prejudice," a number that has increased since 2008, when President Obama was elected.[4]

Certainly we've made progress in the 2000s on the problem of black incarceration—you would think. But there are now nearly one million black people in jails in America: some 43 percent of the total prison population (though blacks constitute only 13.2 percent of the US general population).[5] To highlight the disparity with a single example, consider that even though nearly the same percentage of blacks and whites use marijuana, blacks are three and a half times more likely to be jailed for marijuana possession.[6]

We came to expect a "post-racial" society to blossom during the Obama presidency, but it simply hasn't happened.

The future doesn't look any rosier. Alan Noble suggests that we came to expect a "post-racial" society to blossom during the

Obama presidency, but it simply hasn't happened. Even though the election of the first black president suggested that "we were so over that whole racism thing," Noble writes, "There's good reason to believe that America is more divided over race today than it was the day Obama took office."[7] I don't know that I expected a "post-racial" America, but I think we could have made more progress than we have.

I feel hopeless when all these indicators suggest that the younger generations are as racist as the older ones; when supremacy groups that grow Dylann Roofs are proliferating; when anti-black prejudice is deepening among white people; and when I come to grips with the impact of black incarceration—not just the stats themselves but the devastating truth underlying those numbers that nearly one million black men are not available to be fathers to their children, husbands to their wives, and leaders of their families.

Here is the heart of my feelings of hopelessness: The reality of the racial divide simply deepens the racial divide. The disappearance of black males from their families fuels the further disintegration of the black family. And the absence of black fathers creates black sons who are more likely to grow up to be absent black fathers.

Where do we turn for deliverance? For change? For hope?

. . .

Journalist Ta-Nehisi Coates paints a bleak picture of racism and racial injustice in America. His memoir, *Between the World and Me*, rightly challenges the sentimentality of white people who are too eager for feel-good racial resolution. Coates recounts his interview with a Sunday news show host, during which he tried to explain the ways in which white America is destructive to black people, racism is brutal to the black body, and racial bias is deeply embedded in the fabric of our nation. After Coates had spoken, the interviewer showed a photo of a black boy hugging a white police officer—an image that has been widely distributed—and asked Coates about "hope."[8] Coates writes, "I knew then that I had failed. . . . I was sad for the host and sad for all the people out there watching and reveling in a specious hope."[9]

I agree with Ta-Nehisi Coates that we live in an America that wants to believe in a dream that doesn't exist. I agree that in our search for hope, we tend to reach for what is too easy, sentimental, false, and cheap. I agree that much of white America just wants the black problem to go away, to the degree that some celebrities and politicians, incredibly, claim "there is no racism."[10]

In all this, I feel hopeless. I have no reason to believe that things will change in my lifetime. I believe that peaceful protest can sometimes move the needle, but I also believe that violent protest moves the needle back and usually makes things worse. Most of the time, I believe we take two steps forward . . . and then two steps backward. Often it feels as if not much has changed since my granddaddy's day and my dad's youth.

Coates is far from sentimental in his book, but he is full of passion. Written as a letter to his son, his book swirls around from hopeless exasperation to glimpses of light. A "not-quite-hope" kind of light, but still some light. Ultimately, in his pleading, cynical, urgent voice, his passion turns into love. He needs his son to know.

We may feel hopeless, but we keep trying. At the brink of

> We live in an America that wants to believe in a dream that doesn't exist. . . . In our search for hope, we tend to reach for what is too easy, sentimental, false, and cheap.

despair sometimes, we nevertheless try to tell the story. We look around and see them, feel them: a son, a daughter, a family. And suddenly some slivers of light slice through our hopeless exasperation. We love, after all. We need our children to know.

. . .

Granddaddy died on April 1, 2004. I was drafted by the New England Patriots on April 24. He missed my entry into the NFL by three weeks.

I know that my grandfather would have been proud of me, but I know he also would have ribbed me about the team that picked me. You see, his favorite team was always the Dallas Cowboys. I like to think that, had he lived to see me drafted, my grandfather might have started to root for the Patriots—and later the Browns and then the Saints. But maybe not. Both he and my aunt were die-hard Dallas fans. Even now, when my aunt wishes me well before a game against Dallas, she says, "Now, Benjamin, I hope you have a good game—but I hope y'all lose. Go Cowboys!" Nice.

I remember the day of the NFL draft. The whole family was gathered at my parents' house. Kirsten was there too, although I hadn't yet proposed to her. My dad had gotten cable installed for the sole purpose of watching the draft. I remember the start of the ceremonies and the announcement of the first pick: Eli Manning to the San Diego Chargers. Then other names went up on the board, some of them well-known stars today: Philip Rivers, Ben Roethlisberger, and Larry Fitzgerald. We approached the end of the first round.

And then: "With the thirty-second pick in the 2004 NFL draft, the New England Patriots select . . . Benjamin Watson."

It was an indescribable moment. Though I'd been confident beforehand that I would be drafted, when it actually happened, I couldn't quite believe it. Those words, "NFL draft" and "Patriots select," represented the epitome of a sport that I loved and had worked hard at to excel. And now the defending Super Bowl champions wanted me to play for them.

I realize now that it wasn't just an affirmation of my hard work and determination; it was also a testimony to the perseverance of my grandfather and my father and mother to overcome so much in life, to sacrifice, and to teach me to focus on my opportunities rather than on any disadvantages.

It was a testimony to the perseverance of my grandfather and my father and mother to overcome so much in life, to . . . focus on opportunities rather than on disadvantages.

My dad, with a big smile on his face, grabbed me in a big bear hug. We held each other, laughing with joy. In a moment, though, our laughter gave way to weeping. Perhaps it was the tension that had built up and the sudden release of emotion when I was finally picked. But our tears weren't about that.

Granddaddy wasn't with us anymore.

■ ■ ■

In *The Atlantic*, journalist Ta-Nehisi Coates writes:

I think that those of us who reject divinity, who understand that there is no order, there is no arc, that we are night travelers on a great tundra, that stars can't guide us, will understand that the only work that will matter, will be the work done by us. Or perhaps not. Maybe the very myths I decry are necessary for that work. I don't know. But history is a brawny refutation for that religion brings morality. And I now feel myself more historian than journalist.[11]

I have another view.

I believe in God. Not in a God of religion. Not in the "God" of white supremacy. Not in a white God or a black God. Not in a God of a political party.

I believe in a personal God: the God of the Bible, whose Son, Jesus Christ, is real and who transforms lives by redeeming human hearts. The God who loves me and you, the black person and the white person, and all persons—personally, desperately, sacrificially.

He, too, wrote a memoir.

There is no task in heaven or on earth more difficult than changing the human heart. . . . It requires a supernatural solution.

The problem of race is deep and wide and requires seismic change. But if we look to government to solve it, we might as well feel hopeless. If we look to corporate America to solve it, we'll be waiting a long, long time. And if we agree with Ta-Nehisi Coates, who tentatively suggests that "the only work that will matter, will be the work done by us," then we will truly despair, for we know how well *that* has worked. If we follow that track, we'll quickly add in disbelief, as he did, "Or perhaps not."

As I've said, the problem of race is not "out there." It's "in here," in the human heart. And though there is no task in heaven or on earth more difficult than changing the human heart, I believe in the one who can do it. It requires a supernatural solution.

Yes, I believe in God. You see, I know how God can change a person's heart.

. . .

I wish I could have yet one more moment with my granddaddy.

I'd tell him that I'm playing pro football these days. That I married Kirsten and have five kids. That the first car I bought had a license plate that read WATUSI III. That my football career eventually brought me to New Orleans (which is a lot closer to the Dallas Cowboys, right, Granddaddy?).

I'd tell him I still remember that day we tossed a baseball in his backyard.

I'd tell him I want to hear more about the America he grew up in. About what he faced as a black man. About how he developed the dignity he had within.

I'd tell him about God, because throughout his life he never was a believer—until toward the very end, I am told, when he finally accepted Jesus. I would tell him I'm a follower of Jesus too.

9

HOPEFUL

I'M HOPEFUL
because I know that while we still have race issues
in America, we enjoy a much different normal
than those of our parents and grandparents. I see
it in my personal relationships with teammates,
friends, and mentors. And it's a beautiful thing.

IF POP POP AND GRANDDADDY taught me about race and the history of black people in America, I learned about life from my dad.

I will never forget one time when Daddy and I made a visit to Toys R Us. I was about ten years old, and I don't remember what we bought; but I recall my dad paying at the cash register and receiving his change. As we walked to the car, he counted the money and realized the cashier had given him too much in return.

I was elated. I knew that money wasn't abounding at our house, and I felt like it was our lucky day. It was the clerk's fault, not ours. I felt we should get to keep the money and maybe use it for some ice cream.

My dad and I talked about it, and he didn't see it that way. He said it didn't matter if the lady realized her mistake or not. You do what's right because it's right, not because someone is watching.

We walked back into the store, and he gave the woman the extra money. All three dollars of it. But that's how my dad approached everything. He's a man of principle, not popularity. I'll never forget that day. A lesson in integrity.

It wasn't always that way for my dad, though. His life could've gone in a totally different direction.

. . .

When Kenny Watson was a kid, he quickly developed two ideas about the world. The first was never to trust white people,

171

especially white males. The second was that white people set the parameters for success in life. You couldn't trust white men, yet you had to play their game, abide by their rules, and meet or exceed their standards. Often those standards were arbitrarily weighted against young black kids like Kenny.

Bowling Park Elementary School in 1963 was an all-black school in an all-black Norfolk community. My grandparents were living at Marshall Manor, the affordable-income apartments on the other side of the bridge. My father remembers his second-grade class at Bowling Park, specifically the day when he was asked to get up in front of the class and read a news article. The writer described the tension of the times—mandatory busing of black children into white schools. Seven-year-old Kenny Watson read aloud descriptions of angry white men carrying signs that read, "Nigger Go Home."

> You couldn't trust white men, yet you had to play their game, abide by their rules, and meet or exceed their standards.

My dad says that before that day at Bowling Park Elementary he hadn't thought about how the community he lived in, the school he went to, and the church he attended were all black. His only experience with white people was when two insurance agents knocked on the door once a month to collect payment for a policy. Otherwise, he was like most young kids—aware of race but unaware that it was a problem.

But while reading about angry white men carrying racist signs, Kenny suddenly realized that this was a statement about *him*. And it was a statement *against* him. Soon he would put two and two together—that he was in an all-black school because whites wanted it that way. And soon the nonissue of white and black became a very big, vicious, and hurtful issue, something that filled my dad with pain and anger as a young boy.

The seeming futility and hopelessness of race relations are never more evident than when we see a familiar cycle play itself out over and over: the racialization of boys and girls at very young ages, planting seeds of hate that germinate anger and sprout weeds of violence. We militarize our children, training them to see the world as a racial war.

Within months, Kenny Watson would be placed on the front lines.

Some might ask why my grandparents moved to the white community of Campostella Heights in the early '60s. Some would question whether Granddaddy and Grandma intended to create a problem, whether they meant to force a racial issue. Of course, those were typical questions then, and still are. The mindset of the times assumed a comfortable norm in segregation, and when blacks made an effort to integrate themselves into white society, it was quickly questioned by white people and seen as an act of provocation.

Why should they move there? Why might it be considered wrong for them to move wherever they might choose? These were questions raised only about black people, never about white people.

Knowing my grandparents, their move to Campostella Heights was not about making a point. It was not a racial choice. It was about raising a family, providing my dad and his siblings a house rather than an apartment, getting a better education, and pursuing a better future.

Now in third grade, Kenny found himself in school with white kids and looking for white friends to play with. He missed the old neighborhood, but he got along well with the white kids in Campostella Heights. However, after a while he began to notice that some of his white friends were no longer around to play. One by one, his playmates and buddies disappeared. In fact, they no longer lived in the neighborhood. My dad soon learned why.

Shortly after my grandparents and other black families settled into Campostella Heights, for-sale signs began to pop up around the neighborhood. One here, one there. Then more. And more. Some of the white people were moving out as the black people were moving in. It was the phenomenon known as "white flight."

My grandmother tells the story of an experiment she did around this time: calling a white owner who was selling his house in the neighborhood to inquire about the price. She made sure by the sound of her voice on the phone that he could readily identify her as black. He quoted her a certain price. Sometime later she called him back, speaking in such a way that he would assume she was white. He quoted her a different price, many thousands of dollars cheaper than the first price he'd quoted.

My grandmother wasn't surprised, and the evidence was telling: If you're black, you pay more.

On the other side of a long, wooden footbridge that spanned a marshy lowland, there was another community, known simply as Campostella. While white flight transformed Campostella Heights from an integrated neighborhood into an all-black neighborhood, Campostella remained a white neighborhood. My dad soon found himself playing with black kids on the streets of Campostella Heights but going to an integrated school in the white neighborhood of Campostella.

It was on that bridge between white and black that my dad says he learned a lesson about America.

After school he had to walk past a group of white teenagers who waited on the bridge to taunt and threaten the black kids. Usually they let the black girls pass by, but they stopped the black boys, interrogating and bullying them. They threatened to hit the black kids, throw them off the bridge, or even sexually assault them. Almost every time, they demanded money from the black students to allow them to pass. The threats and taunts were filled with racial slurs. Some days after school, my dad said, he would be detained on the bridge for as long as an hour before being allowed to cross.

The white teens, of course, threatened the black kids with serious harm if they told anyone, so for a long time none of the parents knew. But eventually somebody said something, and soon the school posted teachers and parents on the bridge to ensure the black kids' safety to and from school.

Kenny Watson was terrified by these experiences growing up, and they contributed to the shaping of his attitudes toward white people.

While he was still in grade school, he began listening to the radio broadcasts of the Nation of Islam. These radio programs talked about whites as "devils." They detailed the atrocities that white people had done to black people and black communities. They spoke of black contributions to society, America, and the world.

My dad was deeply influenced by these messages, in part because he was not hearing about black history in school. He says that when he was in sixth grade in 1968, he heard that a white man shot and killed Martin Luther King Jr.: "My teacher gave a lengthy monologue to the class, particularly to the black students, exhorting us that no one should judge an entire race of people because of the conduct of one of its members. As I listened to her, I knew I did not dislike her [for being white]—in reality, she was the teacher I liked the most. But the fact remained: A *white* man had killed Dr. King."

My dad remembers his junior-high history teacher beginning the unit on American history with a discussion of George

175

Washington. There was a picture in the textbook of Washington on a plantation with black kids looking admiringly at him. The caption read, "Washington treated blacks well, and they were happy to live on the plantation with him." As they studied further, my dad says it seemed as if blacks did not really do much. "They seemed content to serve paternalistic white folks who were kind enough to provide for them."

As he looked ahead in the textbook, Kenny saw a unit devoted to black American history and the contributions of blacks to the development of America. He looked forward to studying that section. But when the previous unit was finished, the history teacher said they would skip over the next section and move on. When my dad raised his hand and questioned this, the teacher said that the section on black contributions to American history was "not important."

To my dad, that experience was deeply hurtful and demeaning. "From that day forth," he said, "that teacher became a white male I could not trust."

. . .

Ken Watson is, of course, my dad. But he's also representative of many black people in this country.

We can see in my dad's life the shaping of a young black man, his way of thinking, his distrust of white people, and his growing anger and rage.

We can see in his early life an example of the black kids who get an education about race and difference and self-worth on the streets, in the neighborhoods, and while walking across a bridge. And we observe how they *don't* get an education about race and difference and self-worth from their textbooks, teachers, and schools.

We can see a young boy caught in the clunky machinery of governmental remedies, the desegregation programs that were perhaps necessary and yet so often transported young black kids onto the front lines of racial conflict.

As we search for hope amid all the mess, we are quick to look for better solutions from the government and better remedies for an educational system that so often fails so many.

I can easily climb onto the soapbox about education reform. There is so much I want to say about the problem of how the role of black history is diminished in American education as a whole, and how that contributes especially to the emasculation of black men in our society. White people derive a soaring sense of personal value from the legacy of white historical heroes, and yet that same opportunity has been systematically amputated from black education because it's "not important" to white people.

We can see in my dad's life the shaping of a young black man, his way of thinking, his distrust of white people, and his growing anger and rage.

I want to tell everyone how black history is the backbone of America. How America was built on the backs of slaves. How the Civil War was fought in part because of racial prejudice against the black race but mostly because black slaves were responsible for the economic prosperity of the South.

I want to rejoice in the pantheon of black heroes, showing the ways in which they overcame unspeakable horrors, hateful prejudice, and systemic restraints to emerge triumphant, with dignity as human beings, leading the way to a better world for both blacks and whites.

But then I know I have to get off my hobbyhorse. I realize that hope will not ultimately be found in the educational system or the government. Hope will not be found in programs. Hope will not even be found in learning about the great black people of history.

I believe that hope will be found only in the God of heaven and earth and in the choices we make about him.

. . .

Even as my dad, growing up, developed a distrust of white males and began to grow seeds of resentment toward white people in general, he also had a sense within himself to look at the world honestly.

Despite all the racial taunting he experienced in junior high, and despite his bad experiences with certain teachers, he enjoyed going to school. Many of his white teachers were women, and he got along well with them. He says, "If they held any negative attitudes toward black students, they certainly did a remarkable job of hiding it." My dad recognized that he could learn from white people as well as black people.

He decided at some point that if he were ever going to amount to something, he would have to compete with white people on their terms.

He decided at some point that if he were ever going to amount to anything, he would have to compete with white people on their terms. He developed a perspective by which he would measure himself according to the top standards in the world. When he was selected to compete in a school spelling bee, he wound up going head-to-head with a white student in the finals, and he ultimately won. He competed in athletics as well, starring in football and excelling on the gridiron.

My dad was troubled sometimes by the thought that he was living his life for the approval of whites. But his drive and determination were really more about the standards he set for himself. Ken Watson didn't want to settle for lower expectations just because he was black and others might expect less of him because of it.

Even so, my dad continued to wrestle with the anger and distrust he felt toward white people. When he entered high school, he was bused to Lake Taylor Senior High, a newly built school in a white neighborhood seven miles from his house. Ken Watson began his high school career with caution and a chip on his shoulder.

He made the football team but intentionally remained aloof. He was convinced that the white coaches didn't really care about him. He closed himself off from others and told people he didn't want to be anyone's friend. He says, "I rejected all advances of friendship and would usually give a historical dissertation as to why I remained justified in doing so."

But for all his antipathy toward white people, the greatest struggle he faced was within himself. He recognized his own aimlessness and was bothered by what he perceived as his own lack of purpose. This had nothing to do with being black or white.

It had to do with God.

．　．　．

My father's story is of a young black man caught between hate and acceptance; between white people who cared about him and white people who abused him; between black people who were good to him and black voices broadcasting violence. And somehow in this balance my dad recognized something really important: *truth*.

This portrait of my father as a young man is common—a young black man caught in environments and programs and neighborhoods that conspired to form in him a radical and racial view of the world. And yet his story is not so common either, because it's a picture of a man who somehow found in himself an honesty about his own heart, the world we have, and what was missing.

My father's story is a picture of a man who somehow found in himself an honesty about his own heart, the world we have, and what was missing.

As a teenager, my dad recognized that he was living aimlessly, without purpose. Some paths that he was following were paved with lies. He was discontented, not with the outside world or the white people over there, but with what was coiled up inside his heart. He recognized what was within.

Filled with confusion and distrust and some measure of black anger, my father went outside one summer night and looked up at the sky. Feeling the weight of his own discontentment and dissatisfaction with the aimlessness of his life, he intended to have it out with God. In that moment, he said, he felt himself "overwhelmed by creation."

He cried out, "God, I know you exist. No man put the stars, the moon, or the sun in space. I also know that I don't know you. If you will make a way for me to know you, I will give my life to you."

Immediately, he felt a sense of joy. He felt an assurance that God would answer his prayer. He knew in his heart that God would give him a purpose.

There's a Bible verse that says, "You will know the truth, and the truth will set you free" (John 8:32, NIV). My father's inner discontentment compelled him to pursue the truth, the ultimate truth—and God, the author of all that is true, set him free.

Some time later, my father was watching TV, flipping through the channels. Somehow he landed on a channel featuring a white evangelist, Billy Graham. At one of his crusades in front of thousands, Graham spoke about what the Bible says: very simply, that the root of the problem is sin in our hearts, and that the answer is Jesus Christ, the Son of God, who forgives our sins.

In that divine moment, the young Kenny Watson gave his life to Jesus Christ, and he came face-to-face with real hope.[1]

. . .

I believe that things are better today than they were during my dad's early years in the 1960s, or during Granddaddy's life working at the US Naval Operating Base in Norfolk in the 1940s, or Pop Pop's years in Washington, DC, in the 1930s. We can look back five generations to our ancestors who lived in the time of slavery and during the Civil War. And though the events of the past year in Ferguson and elsewhere are tragic and overwhelming and bring me to moments of despair, I cannot help but feel that some things are different. Some things are better today than they were before.

We have largely overcome the attitudes and practices of the separate-but-equal society. Yes, blacks and whites are still too segregated, but black people are not institutionally separated out, as in the time of Rosa Parks. I don't have to use a separate bathroom for colored people, as my grandparents did early in their lives.

We can go to the restaurants and stores and entertainment venues we want to and not be shut out of American culture and commerce.

We have the right to vote. And we have safe access to the voting booth. We mustn't take that for granted, or else we dismiss the work and sacrifice of so many who marched for voting rights in the 1960s.

White flight is now a much less common practice in our

society. In 1958, 44 percent of whites said they'd move if a black family moved into their neighborhood; by 1998, that number was down to just one percent.[2]

Today, we are far more likely to have friends from a different race than we were in the '60s and earlier. More than four-fifths of blacks claim they have white friends; likewise for white people claiming they have black friends.[3]

I don't overlook the problems that still exist and the pockets of society where sometimes even these marks of progress have not been realized, and yet we must not lose sight of what has been accomplished and how far we've come.

This gives me hope.

I work with white men and black men in the sport of professional football. And though sometimes there are racial issues, for the most part there is understanding and acceptance. Legendary coach Bill Parcells, in his Pro Football Hall of Fame enshrinement speech, reminisced about his experience in the locker room.

> Now, talent aside, we know it's the football business, but the only prerequisite for acceptance into that locker room is you've got to be willing to contribute to the greater good, and if you are willing to do that, you are readily accepted. If you're not, you're pretty much quickly rejected.
>
> Now we've got all kinds in this place. We've got white, we've got black, we've got Latin, we've got Asian, we've got Samoans, we've got Tongans, we've got Native Americans. Ladies and gentlemen, I played and coached with them all, and the only thing that made any difference is are you willing to help? And if you are, come on in. If you're not, get the heck out of here.[4]

This gives me hope.

My dad went on to fulfill his promise to God. He has given his life to Christian ministry, pastoring a church and working with the Fellowship of Christian Athletes. Jesus healed his heart, rescued it from anger and distrust, and gave him a new heart filled with love. The young Kenny Watson went on to seminary to get his Bible education. He had developed a deep knowledge of the Bible already, but he needed his degree. He had no money. But someone paid his way. That person happened to be a white man.

This gives me hope.

■ ■ ■

As I recount my dad's early life, I am deeply aware of how his choices fifty years ago have everything to do with me, what I am, and what my life has turned out to be. It was a long time ago, and yet not such a long time.

By circumstance, I grew up in the same neighborhood where my dad grew up. And though I, too, had to wrestle with racial issues during those years, my dad had already done a lot of the work ahead of me. In spite of the racial divide that still exists there, I can see that much has changed for the better.

I remember when I was in ninth grade at Norfolk Academy, playing football. We were in the Virginia Prep League, and many of the schools were hours apart, spread across the state of Virginia. I was playing varsity, and I was terrified because so many of the guys were bigger than I was.

The week we played at Fork Union Military Academy, which was hours from Norfolk, I was in the starting lineup at safety. It was a rainy day, and the field was a mess. I was miserable and completely out of my league. It got so bad that I spent most of the game acting as if I were trying to make tackles, but I kept slipping on purpose so as not to get run over.

I felt utterly defeated and totally inadequate.

Just then, I heard a voice: "LET'S GO, BENJAMIN!"

I knew that voice. It was my father's. Unbeknownst to me, Daddy had driven the 150 miles to Fork Union and was sitting in the stands in the rain. He'd come just to watch me play. The strength of his voice gave me confidence and made me feel important. Immediately, I started playing differently, with renewed enthusiasm. After the game, my dad drove home to be ready to preach a sermon in church the next morning.

> Daddy's story will never appear in a textbook of black history, but he's a hero nonetheless. He's *my* hero. And his voice echoes through the years.

Daddy's story will never appear in a textbook of black history, but he's a hero nonetheless. He's *my* hero. And his voice echoes through the years, cheering me on, giving me confidence, and making me feel important.

I think this is also true about God the Father. When we are flopping around in the mud of life and race, feeling utterly defeated and totally inadequate, he is there. When we finally look to the heavens and call out to him, he is there. And even when, perhaps, we are not listening for his voice because we're so caught up in our circumstances, we hear him say, "Let's go."

This gives me hope.

ENCOURAGED

I'M ENCOURAGED
because ultimately the problem is not a
SKIN problem, it is a SIN problem.
SIN is the reason we rebel against authority.
SIN is the reason we abuse our authority.
SIN is why we are racist and prejudiced and
why we lie to cover for our own.
SIN is the reason we riot, loot, and burn.

But I'M ENCOURAGED
because God has provided a solution for sin through
his son, Jesus, and with it, a transformed heart and
mind. One that's capable of looking past the outward
and seeing what's truly important in every human
being. The cure for the Michael Brown, Trayvon
Martin, Tamir Rice, and Eric Garner tragedies
is not education or exposure. It's the gospel.

So, finally, I'M ENCOURAGED
because the gospel gives mankind hope.

WHEN I WROTE the Facebook post after the Ferguson grand jury decision was announced, it opened a lot of doors with my teammates. Many of the players and coaches, black and white, told me, "That's what I was thinking; I just didn't know how to say it."

Ferguson wasn't just Ferguson. It was America. It was the symbol of so many racial conflicts over the months—each with different sets of circumstances, all of them prompting strong responses among blacks and whites.

It's hard to follow current events closely during the NFL season. Football can be like a bottomless pit, consuming everyone involved for six months. Ferguson, though, was something none of us could get away from. I suspect this was true for most Americans—the nature of the Ferguson tragedy galvanized the attention of people who would otherwise be wrapped up in their own work and daily pursuits. It was on the news constantly, from August (when Michael Brown was killed) through November (when a grand jury decided there was not enough probable evidence to indict Officer Darren Wilson).

For us ballplayers—in my case, on the New Orleans Saints— some things are still hard to talk about, despite how close we become during training camp and the regular season. As the saying goes: If you want to keep friends, never talk about religion or politics. Or race.

But my Facebook post opened the conversation among us.

Even if we didn't agree totally—and we often didn't—we could at least express our views and hear from each other. I heard every kind of opinion from all sides of the spectrum. But it was encouraging that almost every response became a *dialogue*.

> It was encouraging that almost every response became a *dialogue*. Sometimes we had to agree to disagree, but that was after a back-and-forth discussion.

Sometimes we had to agree to disagree, but that was after a back-and-forth discussion. Talking about these issues is the first step to understanding and healing.

One teammate asked me, "Did you write something important? My mom just told me I had to read something written by one of my teammates."

The feedback I received from the public via Facebook, Twitter, and e-mail mirrored what I'd heard from my friends and teammates. One person, identifying himself as an atheist, commented at the end of my post. He thanked me for my words, which he truly appreciated, "minus the part about God."

I appreciated his response and told him so.

But there can never be a "minus the part about God" if we want real solutions.

▪ ▪ ▪

I think it's interesting that so many people agree that the tragedy at the Charleston AME church, where Dylann Roof shot nine people to death, was pure evil. I don't know how we can quickly agree on the presence of evil but still question the existence of God.

I believe in God, and I don't know how we can talk about the race problem in America without talking about God.

What is under our skin, and under the skin problem in America, is a spiritual problem. Every time we point at someone else or at an entire race—reducing them to a single story, diminishing them by stereotypes and assumptions—we overlook our own failure. When we point outside ourselves and say, "You should have done this . . ." or "You were wrong to . . ." we miss the point.

When we focus on another person's *skin*, we miss the reality of our own *sin*.

This is not about religion or church. This is about you and me, black and white, individually acknowledging that we have done wrong. That we have judged others. That we have bias and prejudice in our own hearts.

It starts *here*.

Indeed, that very idea is found in the Bible: "Everyone has sinned; we all fall short of God's glorious standard" (Romans 3:23, NLT). One thing I am absolutely certain of: Darren Wilson is a sinner, and so was Michael Brown. So am I. And so are you.

This race business must grieve God greatly. From his perspective, it's not about white or black, fair or unfair, or statistics about the police or black people. From God's perspective, we have *all* messed up, and we're *all* in need of him.

> **This is not about religion or church. This is about you and me, black and white, individually acknowledging that we have done wrong.**

God gives *race* a new meaning. It's called the *human* race.

. . .

Here's what I've come to believe: At the root of racism is a flawed view of ourselves.

Racism is based on an elevation of our own talents, physical characteristics, and DNA—which we inherited by no choice or merit of our own—over someone else's. It's an assumption that the other person is *different* and thus we are better. It's an attitude that says, "*I* represent the norm, and *you* are the variation, the outlier, the odd one."

It's wrong, of course—not just morally but factually. As I have written here, we all—black, white, Hispanic, Asian, Native American, and every other race—are 99.9 percent the same. We all have predominantly the same DNA. We all are human.

I recently had an appointment with a dermatologist. I sat in the examination room and checked my iPhone as I waited for the doctor to come in. After a short wait, I heard the customary knock, the door opened slowly, and in walked my new dermatologist.

I'm not sure what I expected, but the doctor turned out to be a brown-haired white woman who was a little older than I am. We exchanged background information for a few minutes. She was very knowledgeable and knew just what to do to help me.

At the end of the visit, I asked her a question about a specific hair product she had recommended. I must have known it was a borderline dumb question, so I prefaced it with, "Excuse my ignorance, but . . . with these products, does it matter if you're black or white?"

What she said next reminded me of what I already know but constantly need to be reminded of.

"Hair is just hair," she said. "It's all about texture, and that depends on the melanin in your skin. Under a microscope, all skin and hair follicles are basically the same. The only difference is the amount of melanin. Curl types and hair properties such as texture, density, elasticity, and porosity can vary across the spectrum of skin tone. So really, hair is about the individual, not the individual's race."

It's amazing that melanin—the pigment that gives human skin, hair, and eyes their color—has caused so much pain and tragedy in America.

Race is indeed a figment of our melanin. Our differences are cultural, not genetic. Across the globe, we have different marriage customs, languages, dress, and diets. Even with all these differences, our DNA is extremely similar. So when our God-given differences make us think we are somehow better than others, we must reevaluate the foolishness of our thinking.

> Race is indeed a figment of our melanin. Our differences are cultural, not genetic.

When black neurosurgeon Dr. Ben Carson was asked why he doesn't talk about race more often, he said, "When I take someone into the operating room, I'm actually operating on the thing [the brain] that makes them who they are. The skin doesn't make them who they are."[1]

Under our skin, we are the same—flesh, blood, and spirit. We are commonly human. All of us are human beings, whom God created.

. . .

The good news is that we all are human. The bad news is that all humans have the same disease. It's called sin.

Because we all descended from the first man, Adam, we inherited his sin nature from birth. People often say that kids have to learn to be bad. But as a father of five, I can tell you that they are sinful as soon as they get here. It may take some time to fully manifest, but every child is selfish, prideful, jealous, and rebellious. And the condition doesn't cure itself when we become adults. Our sin nature is alive from day one and continues to keep us in bondage, compelling us to succumb to its desires.

So when we talk about justice, we need to be mindful of the justice that *we* deserve in the eyes of God.

I think it's interesting that so many people are quick to point out other people's wrongdoing and yet are resistant to using the word *sin*. Why is that? Maybe we know that deep down, we are sinful ourselves. If we use the word *sin*, we implicate ourselves.

We point our finger at Michael Brown for stealing a cigarillo. But if we used the word *sin*, we might have to fess up about cheating on our taxes or stealing from our employers. Yes, we cheat and steal in other ways and then lie to say we haven't. We are fornicators, adulterers, and abusers. We are racists.

We are sinners.

The soil that racism grows from is sin.

At times, our plight can seem hopeless, and our efforts to change can seem futile. The beauty of the gospel (the good news about God) is that he loved us so much that he sent his Son as a sacrificial redeemer, not only to pay the penalty for our sin (through his death) but also to free us from the bondage of sin and give us everlasting life. What we need runs so much deeper than a cure for a single social ill. We need a cure for the common sin, the central obstacle that separates us from God.

> **What we need runs so much deeper than a cure for a single social ill. We need a cure for the common sin, the central obstacle that separates us from God.**

It is only by the power of God that our hearts can be transformed from the inside out.

It is only by the power of God that changed hearts will produce changed behavior and a changed society.

．．．

There is something else important here that we cannot afford to overlook.

Grace.

Many people know about grace through the hymn "Amazing

Grace," which is often thought to be a Negro spiritual. But it was written by a white British poet and pastor named John Newton.

Earlier in his life, in the mid-1700s, Newton was a slave trader. He transported slaves on ships from Africa to—get this—Charleston, South Carolina. He was an atheist, convinced that if there was a God, this God wasn't making himself known to one John Newton.

On one transatlantic crossing, Newton's ship encountered a terrible storm. Everyone on board thought they were doomed. In the turmoil, Newton prayed—and God made himself known to him. The ship survived, the journey was completed, and John Newton found faith in God.

In his later life, Newton became an abolitionist, fighting against the institution of slavery. And he wrote the famous hymn that begins, "Amazing grace! how sweet the sound—that saved a wretch like me!" The hymn was later sung by slaves in America.

But my point about grace doesn't concern the hymn. It concerns the changed heart of the person who wrote it. Grace is about how God bridges the racial divide one heart and one person at a time.

Throughout this book, we've talked about this person or that person who did something wrong and became part of the national conversation surrounding a racial incident. We say this person deserves this and that person deserves that. We call for justice to be done. Yet we fail to see our own sin and the justice *we* deserve because of it.

> We call for justice to be done. Yet we fail to see our own sin and the justice *we* deserve because of it.

The equation of God's justice is this: our sin = punishment and death.

So we all—black human beings and white human beings alike—must come to recognize our own sin. We must understand the just punishment we deserve. We must come to a place of personal brokenness and see our need—our desperate need—for God.

The Bible says: "If we confess our sins, he is faithful and just and will forgive us our sins and purify us from all unrighteousness" (1 John 1:9, NIV).

Here is the equation of the salvation that God offers us: our confession of sin + faith in Jesus Christ = forgiveness and deliverance.

If and when we confess, through repentance and faith we will discover grace—the grace of God that says we are forgiven.

And here's the point: Only when we personally experience God's grace—his unmerited favor—will we be able to extend grace to others. To Darren Wilson. To Michael Brown. To each other as black and white human beings.

This is the gospel. The Good News. The apostle Paul, writing in the first century, said, "There is neither Jew nor Greek, there is neither slave nor free, there is no male and female, for you are all one in Christ Jesus" (Galatians 3:28, ESV).

I am not naive enough to believe that the issue of race will be totally eradicated from our midst while we're here on planet Earth. Until Christ returns, there will always be bastions of hatred and callousness.

I'm encouraged, though, because the times we're living in have forced us to be honest about where we stand, priming us for God to do a tremendous work in our lives, if we'll let him. As black people and white people, we need that revival, that awakening. And it can happen through Jesus Christ.

Only through a relationship with Jesus Christ will the earthly distinctions between us fade, as our oneness in him takes precedence over color, creed, and culture and as our allegiance to him compels us to make those who matter to him matter most to us.

This is our hope.

EMPOWERED

In the aftermath of Ferguson and Charleston and Baltimore and so many other incidents and tragedies, I feel EMPOWERED to act out my faith in ways that can bridge the racial divide.

THIS STATEMENT wasn't part of my original Facebook post, but it needs to be part of our ongoing mission and calling.

Yes, acknowledging our own sin, repenting, and experiencing God's grace in our lives are the first steps in bridging the racial divide. We won't change the world *around* us unless God has changed the world *within* us. But that's just the first step.

The Bible tells us that "faith without works is dead" (James 2:20, KJV), which means that God's work within us should prompt us to act out the gospel in the world around us.

But what should we do about the racial divide? What *can* we do?

One problem I see is the potential for doing good things for the wrong reasons. Often when people reach a hand across the racial aisle, it's a gesture that serves to make themselves feel good, rather than to effect real change. Other times when we do a good thing, it can be for show—something we do only because it looks good to others. We don't accomplish anything by creating false and sentimental kids-hugging-cops pictures. These "works" lack integrity and truth.

> Often when people reach a hand across the racial aisle, it's a gesture that serves to make them feel good, rather than to effect real change.

No, any meaningful change we might pursue requires a willingness to engage *personally*, over time, getting our hands dirty in the mess of it all. This isn't a one-time appearance. It's an ongoing involvement.

I certainly don't have all the answers, but I have some ideas. The way I think about it, there are four arenas of change that a person might focus on in his or her life: *personal, family, church,* and *nation.*

. . .

I believe the racial problem of "us versus them" continues because there is an "us" and there is a "them."

What if there were just an "us"? What if we made it personal by doing more to erase the racial divide in our own lives? What if we sought intentional relationships with people who are not of our race?

The key to this idea is the word *intentional*. Because America is still significantly segregated, there aren't always natural opportunities to make friends with someone of another race. And because of the great disparity between the number of whites and blacks, the natural opportunities for a white person to make friends with a black person are more limited. It will require both groups to make an intentional effort.

We cannot and should not try to force friendships, but friendships can be intentionally sought and cultivated. If we don't have friends of another race, it's usually because we haven't tried.

We may need to become more intentional about making friends across racial lines at work, where those opportunities exist. We could do so through the schools where our children attend. Or maybe by volunteering on community projects where whites and blacks can work side by side. Maybe by attending a more racially diverse church, or one that is predominantly a different race from your own.

I'm aware that some research suggests that forging white-black friendships doesn't show a statistical improvement in the racial divide. But I have to think it's because there's not enough of it happening. I also think that sometimes those relationships are too superficial and contrived. We cannot and should not try to force friendships, but friendships can be intentionally sought and cultivated. If we don't have friends of another race, it's usually because we haven't tried.

When we become genuinely close to someone of a different race, I believe it's easier to understand their perspective. This has certainly been true on the football teams I've played for. Even in the context of Ferguson and my Facebook post, we've agreed on more things than we've disagreed. And that happened because of friendly conversations in the context of relationships forged from mutual pursuits and interests. Friendship is a great way to build understanding and acceptance.

But there's another side to the story as well. As we look to create positive relationships, we must also examine our lives for negative relationships, and we must consider what to do about them. For example, in the presence of a friend or relative who makes racist remarks, do we have the courage to call them on it? Maybe we could say, "I have a friend who is black, and it offends me when you say things like that." Or perhaps, "I have white friends and they are nothing like what you're saying." Do we have that kind of personal courage?

The Bible says that "bad company corrupts good morals."[1] If I willfully surround myself with people who are angry, deceitful, vulgar, rebellious, and racist, I can expect my behavior in some way to follow suit. If the company I keep believes that white people can't be trusted or black people are lazy, and makes jokes and comments to that effect, I will be influenced by their prejudice. My morals will be corrupted. I will become like them.

Do you want to be like that? Really? Ultimately, we may need to separate ourselves from relationships in which racism is perpetuated. Some relationships may need to be intentionally broken.

I realize this is difficult when racism runs deep in families. Taking a stand is tough when it's against your brother or sister, mother or father. Then again, taking a stand is really as much about *your* character as theirs. What are you willing to stand up for? Maybe there's an opportunity to make a positive difference.

. . .

Our children and grandchildren are the legacy we will leave to the world—our memorial to a time we will never see.

The children of today will steer the culture of tomorrow. We have a limited number of years—the blink of an eye, really—to teach them right from wrong. They absorb our every look, comment, and action. When the subject is race, they model themselves after us. When the next racial incident happens on the news, they can predict our reaction, our attitude, before we even respond.

> **The children of today will steer the culture of tomorrow. We have a limited number of years . . . to teach them right from wrong.**

When the video of Eric Garner's arrest was released, my daughter walked in while I was watching it unfold on CNN. Subsequently, she's seen glimpses of racial protests on television, and they have prompted her to pray for Baltimore and Charleston every night since those incidents occurred.

Yes, I am proud of her. Yes, I know her response in some way echoes what she's seen in me. And yes, it's sobering to realize that she has picked up so many things from me in so many areas of life.

As a parent, I am the shepherd of my child's heart, and I must discern what he or she should be exposed to, and when. In all these things Kirsten and I have been honest with our kids, giving them the facts and not just our opinions. I acknowledge that my opinions are sometimes untrue and biased; I don't want what I think to influence them in a negative way.

I know very well how difficult it is for parents to know the right course of action when such sensitive issues are unfolding right before our eyes. Yet as challenging as these conversations may be, they may also be great opportunities to steer our children toward the bridge across the racial divide. It's certainly a way to emphasize how, as human beings, we all fall short and need redemption and healing. As my daughter prays for forgiveness to reign supreme in Baltimore and Charleston, I cannot help but be challenged to show my children that their daddy needs forgiveness too.

The final scene in *A Time to Kill* sticks in my mind's eye: that moment when the white family of lawyer Jake Brigance and the black family of Carl Lee Hailey sit down together at a picnic.

What would happen if we followed their example? What would happen if we made that story into nonfiction?

■   ■   ■

Not long ago, my friend Chris made the intentional decision to attend a black church.

For years, he and his family have been part of a predominantly white evangelical megachurch, and they continue to attend there much of the time. But Chris became convicted that he and his wife and kids should experience a church that was predominantly black.

"I didn't attend there with any intention to help anyone or to do a good thing for the racial problem," he said. "I just wanted to know what it was like."

Somewhat to his surprise, he found it deeply meaningful and very enjoyable. He spoke of the passion of black worship, the power of the message, and the intensity and vibrancy of the music. They went back the next week and have continued to participate on other occasions. Though Chris and his family are still committed to their regular congregation, he now looks forward to attending the black church from time to time and building some relationships there.

I wonder what would happen if a white church and black church partnered together in a Bible study. If white men and black men came together in a regular small group to talk about families and marriages and work and challenges and triumphs. If white women and black women came together in a small group to study the Word of God. I know this happens sometimes. Why can't we make it happen more often?

> I wonder what would happen if . . . white men and black men came together in a regular small group to talk about families and marriages and work and challenges and triumphs.

Unfortunately, our churches remain largely segregated. I know that church planting is often directed by demographic research—population studies that may or may not categorize by race (though I hope not). But I can well imagine that these demographic studies rarely place a new church into a mixed-race neighborhood.

But one church that did has had a positive impact on the city of St. Louis, Missouri.

Apostles Church was planted on Delmar Boulevard—a street known locally as the Delmar Divide—in a neighborhood that features wealth on the south side and poverty on the north. These neighborhoods are also racially divided—70 percent white to the south and 98 percent black to the north.

Todd Genteman, the pastor of Apostles Church and a church planter for the Missouri Baptist Convention, says, "Discipleship is one way to bridge the divide. We need to stand with Jesus and break down the dividing walls of hostility. The progression of the gospel is multi-ethnic worship: every tribe and every nation worshiping together. It's timely in our city. It's part of our church's passion, and it's the theological truth of the Bible."[2]

It's encouraging that some churches are conceived and built this way. It's discouraging that there aren't more congregations like Apostles Church.

It's encouraging that the power of the gospel can bring white people and black people together in Christ. It's discouraging that the church so often stands in the way.

■ ■ ■

The problem of race in America is a spiritual problem at the heart of America.

Individually we may feel as if there's not much we can do. But maybe we underestimate what God can do *through* us.

I believe it's essential for us to pray for America. I know there are some who hear that and think it's a soft solution to a hard racial problem. On the contrary—prayer is one of the most powerful and pragmatic actions we can take to overcome racism in America.

> Individually we may feel as if there's not much we can do. But maybe we underestimate what God can do *through* us.

Prayer has often ignited revival. Spiritual awakenings have exploded out of prayer meetings where even a few people have dedicated themselves to pray for their families, communities, and nation. It has happened before. It can happen again.

So, I urge everyone to pray.

Pray for the families of the victims and the perpetrators.

Pray for our communities and cities, that tensions will cease.

Pray for the people we think are at fault and the ones we know are at fault.

Pray for direction—that God would specifically guide you into action.

Pray for wisdom for those who make decisions and laws.

Pray for the safety of law enforcement officers and the eradication of the lawlessness they are commissioned to fight.

Pray that we all will be keenly aware of our thoughts and reactions and will be bold enough to apologize when we should.

Pray for the courage to stand up against racism wherever it's found—and especially when it is expressed by friends and family.

Pray for courage to call wrong *wrong* and right *right*.

Pray for God's healing hand on America.

"Be strong and take heart, all you who hope in the Lord" (Psalm 31:24, NIV).

ACKNOWLEDGMENTS

DECIDING TO WRITE A BOOK is no small undertaking, especially for someone who has never done it before. It's one thing to write down my reflections in a blog; it's another to fill the pages of a book. Although this book is directly tied to my thoughts about Ferguson, it is filled with a lifetime of observations and reflections from relationships I've had since birth. This project would never have come to fruition had it not been for several important people. In thanking these people, I will start with my most recent relationships and work my way back.

I must start by saying thank you to my writer, Ken Petersen, for his incredible work on this project in such a short time. Thanks for helping me organize my thoughts, notes, and ramblings, and for challenging me to dig deeper when needed. Your writing, ideas, and contributions made my first book-writing process a joy.

A big thank you to Jan, Todd, Nancy, and the Tyndale Momentum publishing team for enthusiastically catching the vision for this book and your commitment to making it a success.

Thank you to DJ Snell of Legacy Management and Mark Lepselter of Maxx Sports & Entertainment for guiding me through this process. DJ, you have been patient with my questions explaining every detail and helping me be confident as I navigated unknown territory. Mark, I've relied on your experience and insight in this arena from Day One.

I would not have had the opportunity to write this had it not been for the churches, public and private organizations, universities, television networks, and print media that responded to my words and invited me to engage with them. And these meetings would never have been realized without Ansley Fous and EAG Sports Management constantly fielding requests and searching for new opportunities. Thank you for your dedication to my family and me.

There are some who say that athletes should just play their sport and leave the comments about politics, religion, and social issues to others. Thank you to the hundreds of thousands of people who allow me and other athletes to express their thoughts about the issues that affect all of us. It has been encouraging and overwhelming to hear feedback and read your comments. Thank you for allowing me to be a part of your conversations.

Thank you to my teammates (current and former) and friends, some of whose stories are in this book, and who have read what I have written and keep asking me if they will get a copy of this book. Yes! Being comfortable enough to converse and even argue about race, while continuing to respect each other and remain friends, is something I do not take for granted.

To my home-church families: Faith Community Church, Urban Community Church of Norfolk, and Rock Hill Bible Fellowship Church, thank you for teaching me and the other young people about race, and life in general, from a biblical perspective, and for trying to demonstrate what it means to love people with the love of Christ regardless of skin tone, economic status, or educational level.

This book is as much about family as it is about society. Thank you to my grandparents, aunts, uncles, and mother and father for paving the way, defying the odds, enduring hardship, and leaving a legacy of faith for me to follow. Your perseverance made the writing of this book possible. To my five siblings, Jessica, Matthew, Asa, Karis, and Joel, thank you for supporting my endeavors, including this one, and for our candid, late-night conversations about this topic.

To my five children, Grace, Naomi, Isaiah, Judah, and Eden, the innocent beauty of your faces made writing this book even more important. Thank you for your hugs and kisses that always seem to put things into proper perspective. Your generation will carry the torch further, and I cannot wait to see what God does in and through you.

Proverbs 18:22 says, "He who finds a wife finds a good thing and obtains favor from the Lord." Thank you, Kirsten, for being a prayerful, comforting, encouraging, strong, and loving wife. You always challenge my "Why?" with "Why not?" and you see greatness in me that I sometimes don't see in myself. Thank you for always standing beside me. (And thank you for getting me that new computer and desk. You were right. I needed them both!)

Finally, I must thank God for this new and exciting chapter in my life and for giving me the chance to express the things he's made me aware of over the course of my life. May I be faithful with the opportunity he has given me.

NOTES

CHAPTER 1: ANGRY

1. Douglas A. Blackmon, *Slavery by Another Name: The Re-enslavement of Black People in America from the Civil War to World War II* (New York: Doubleday, 2008).
2. Richard Wolf, "Court Faults Redistricting Plan That 'Packed' Black Voters," *USA Today,* March 25, 2015, www.usatoday.com/story/news /nation/2015/03/25/supreme-court-political-redistricting/21698137. Accessed April 6, 2015.
3. Reniqua Allen, "Our 21st-Century Segregation: We're Still Divided by Race," *The Guardian*, April 3, 2013, www.theguardian.com/comment isfree/2013/apr/03/21st-century-segregation-divided-race. Accessed March 31, 2015.
4. Garrett Epps, "Is Racial Segregation Legal, If It's Not Deliberate?" *The Atlantic*, January 22, 2015, www.theatlantic.com/politics/archive /2015/01/is-racial-segregation-constitutional-if-its-not-deliberate /384739. Accessed April 1, 2015.
5. Bob Smietana, "Sunday Morning Segregation: Most Worshipers Feel Their Church Has Enough Diversity," Christianity Today, January 15, 2015, www.christianitytoday.com/gleanings/2015/january/sunday -morning-segregation-most-worshipers-church-diversity.html?paging =off. Accessed March 30, 2015.
6. "Americans Say They Like Diverse Communities; Election, Census Trends Suggest Otherwise," Pew Research Center's *Social Demographic Trends*, December 1, 2008, www.pewsocialtrends.org/2008/12/02 /americans-say-they-like-diverse-communities-election-census -trends-suggest-otherwise. Accessed August 28, 2015.
7. Bruce Drake, "Incarceration Gap Widens between Whites and Blacks," Pew Research Center, September 6, 2013, www.pewresearch.org/fact -tank/2013/09/06/incarceration-gap-between-whites-and-blacks -widens. Accessed March 31, 2015.

CHAPTER 2: INTROSPECTIVE

1. Patricia G. Ramsey, "Early Childhood Multicultural Education," in *Handbook of Research on the Education of Young Children*, second edition, ed. Bernard Spodek and Olivia N. Saracho (New York: Routledge, 2013), 286.
2. Ibid.
3. Mike Johnston's letter is quoted in Lynn Bartels, "After South Carolina, 'This White Man,' Sen. Mike Johnston, Writes a Letter to a Black Denver Church," *The Spot* (blog), *Denver Post*, June 18, 2015, http://blogs.denverpost.com/thespot/2015/06/18/after-south-carolina-this-white-man-sen-mike-johnston-writes-a-letter-to-a-black-denver-church/121286. Accessed August 5, 2015.
4. Ibid.
5. Associated Press, "Representatives of Charleston Shooting Victims 'Forgive' Dylann Roof," *The Guardian*, June 19, 2015, http://www.theguardian.com/world/2015/jun/19/charleston-south-carolina-shooting-dylann-roof-victims-statements. See also "Dylann Roof Bond Hearing. Victims Address Charleston Shooter In Court," YouTube video, www.youtube.com/watch?v=e26Eysq22Yg. Alana Simmons identifies herself at 3:53 and her statement begins at 3:58. Accessed on August 25, 2015.
6. Associated Press, "Representatives of Charleston Shooting Victims 'Forgive' Dylann Roof."

CHAPTER 3: EMBARRASSED

1. Christopher Klein, "Selma's 'Bloody Sunday,' Fifty Years Ago," *History in the Headlines*, March 5, 2015, www.history.com/news/selmas-bloody-sunday-50-years-ago. Accessed August 26, 2015. In the embedded video at the beginning of the article, the mention of the Confederate flag on the front of the state trooper car begins at 1:46.
2. "Confrontations for Justice: John Lewis—March from Selma to Montgomery, 'Bloody Sunday,' 1965," *Eyewitness: American Originals from the National Archives*, the National Archives, http://www.archives.gov/exhibits/eyewitness/html.php?section=2. Accessed August 6, 2015.
3. "Selma to Montgomery March," History.com; www.history.com/topics/black-history/selma-montgomery-march. Accessed August 6, 2015.
4. Ibid.
5. Nicolaus Mills, "King and Johnson after Selma," *Dissent*, February 17, 2015, www.dissentmagazine.org/blog/king-and-johnson-after-selma. Accessed August 31, 2015.
6. Ibid.
7. Kathleen Parker, "The Media Circus around Ferguson," *Washington Post*, December 2, 2014, www.washingtonpost.com/opinions/kathleen-parker-the-media-circus-around-ferguson/2014/12/02/94b42482-7a64-11e4-9a27-6fdbc612bff8_story.html. Accessed July 24, 2015.

8. P. R. Rich and M. S. Zaragoza, "The Continued Influence of Implied and Explicitly Stated Misinformation in News Reports," abstract, *Journal of Experimental Psychology: Learning, Memory, and Cognition*, July 6, 2015 (e-pub ahead of print), www.ncbi.nlm.nih.gov/pubmed/26147670. Accessed July 30, 2015.

9. Eric Horowitz, "How Speculating Newscasters Keep Us Less Informed," *Pacific Standard*, July 29, 2015, www.psmag.com/books-and-culture/how-speculating-newscasters-keep-us-less-informed. Accessed July 30, 2015.

10. Ibid.

11. Josh Levs, "One Challenge for Ferguson Grand Jury: Some Witnesses' Credibility," CNN.com, updated December 14, 2014, www.cnn.com /2014/12/14/justice/ferguson-witnesses-credibility. Accessed on August 26, 2015.

12. "National Bar Association Critical of Ferguson Grand Jury Process," *Here and Now*, November 24, 2014, http://hereandnow.wbur.org/2014 /11/26/ferguson-grand-jury-meanes. Accessed August 30, 2015.

13. Maria L. La Ganga, Tina Susman, and Molly Hennessy-Fiske, "Ferguson Grand Jury Faced Confusing, Contradictory Information," *Los Angeles Times*, November 25, 2014, www.latimes.com/nation/la-na -ferguson-jury-20141125-story.html. Accessed August 30, 2015.

14. *Department of Justice Report Regarding the Criminal Investigation into the Shooting Death of Michael Brown by Ferguson, Missouri Police Officer Darren Wilson*, March 4, 2015, www.justice.gov/sites/default/files/opa /press-releases/attachments/2015/03/04/doj_report_on_shooting_of_ michael_brown_1.pdf. Accessed August 31, 2015.

15. Ken Ham, "Are There Really Different Races?" *Answers in Genesis*, September 16, 2014, https://answersingenesis.org/racism/are-there-really -different-races. Accessed August 30, 2015. Ham cites J. C. Gutin, "End of the Rainbow," *Discover*, pp. 72–73, November 1994; and S. C. Cameron and S. M. Wycoff, "The Destructive Nature of the Term *Race*: Growing beyond a False Paradigm," *Journal of Counseling & Development*, 76:277–285, 1998.

16. Ashley Montagu, *Man's Most Dangerous Myth: The Fallacy of Race*, 6th edition (Walnut Creek, CA: AltaMira Press, 1997), 41.

17. Quoted in "Race in a Genetic World," *Harvard Magazine*, May–June 2008, http://harvardmagazine.com/2008/05/race-in-a-genetic-world -html#. Accessed July 16, 2015.

18. Ibid.

19. Kathy Lohr, "Poor People's Campaign: A Dream Unfulfilled," NPR, June 19, 2008, http://www.npr.org/templates/story/story.php?storyId= 91626373. Accessed August 6, 2015.

CHAPTER 4: FRUSTRATED

1. Judith Smith. "Music and Mood: A Hormone Connection?" *ResearchMatters*, September 29, 2008, https://researchmatters.asu.edu/stories/music-and -mood-hormone-connection-774. Accessed July 31, 2015.

2. Myriam V. Thoma, et al., "The Effect of Music on the Human Stress Response," *PLOS One*, August 5, 2013, http://journals.plos.org/plosone /article?id=10.1371/journal.pone.0070156. Accessed September 1, 2015.

3. 1 John 2:16, NIV

4. Chakara Conyers, "What Hip-Hop Says to a Young Black Woman," RapRehab.com, March 18, 2013, http://raprehab.com/what-hip-hop -says-to-a-young-black-woman. Accessed August 1, 2015.

5. "Essay on Rock and Roll Lyrics," accessed August 1, 2015, http://www .rockwisdom.com/commentaries/essay2.htm.

6. Nathan DeWall, interview by Michele Norris, "Study: Narcissism on Rise in Pop Lyrics," *All Things Considered* (blog), NPR Music, April 26, 2011, www.npr.org/2011/04/26/135745227/study-narcissism-on-rise -in-pop-lyrics. Accessed August 1, 2015. Italics added.

CHAPTER 5: FEARFUL AND CONFUSED

1. Bruce Drake, "Divide between Blacks and Whites on Police Runs Deep," *FactTank* (blog), Pew Research Center, April 28, 2015, http:// www.pewresearch.org/fact-tank/2015/04/28/blacks-whites-police. Accessed August 4, 2015.

2. Patrick O'Connor, "Poll Shows Big Racial Gap in View of Police," *Washington Wire* (blog), *Wall Street Journal*, September 9, 2014, http:// blogs.wsj.com/washwire/2014/09/09/poll-shows-big-racial-gap-in -view-of-police. Accessed August 4, 2015.

3. Nikole Hannah-Jones, "A Letter from Black America," *Politico*, March/April 2015, www.politico.com/magazine/story/2015/03/letter -from-black-america-police-115545.html#.VckWSflVhBe. Accessed August 10, 2015.

4. Ibid.

5. Ibid.

6. Dara Lind, "The Ugly History of Racist Policing in America," *Vox* interview with Heather Ann Thompson, updated on April 27, 2015, www.vox.com/michael-brown-shooting-ferguson-mo/2014/8/19/ 6031759/ferguson-history-riots-police-brutality-civil-rights. Accessed August 4, 2015.

7. Douglas A. Blackmon, *Slavery by Another Name: The Re-enslavement of Black People in America from the Civil War to World War II* (New York: Doubleday, 2008), 3.

8. Franklin Hughes, "Question of the Month: The African Dodger," Jim Crow Museum of Racist Memorabilia, October 1, 2012, http:// www.ferris.edu/jimcrow/question/oct12/index.htm. Accessed August 4, 2015.

9. Drew Griffin and Scott Bronstein, "Video Shows White Teens Driving Over, Killing Black Man, Says DA," CNN, August 8, 2011, http://www .cnn.com/2011/CRIME/08/06/mississippi.hate.crime. Accessed August 27, 2015.

10. Stratton Lawrence, "Walter Scott 'Hunted Down Like a Deer,'" *The Daily Beast*, April 9, 2015, www.thedailybeast.com/articles/2015/04/09 /walter-scott-hunted-down-like-a-deer.html. Accessed August 4, 2015.

11. Juan Forero, "Serial Rapist Gets 155 Years; Judge Suggests His Crimes Contributed to Diallo Shooting," *New York Times*, August 2, 2000, www.nytimes.com/2000/08/02/nyregion/serial-rapist-gets-155-years -judge-suggests-his-crimes-contributed-diallo.html. Accessed August 28, 2015.

12. Rich Juzwiak and Aleksander Chan, "Unarmed People of Color Killed by Police, 1999–2014," *Gawker*, December 8, 2014, http://gawker.com /unarmed-people-of-color-killed-by-police-1999-2014-1666672349. Accessed August 11, 2015.

13. Ryan Gabrielson, Ryann Grochowski Jones, and Eric Sagara, "Deadly Force, in Black and White," *ProPublica*, October 10, 2014, http://www .propublica.org/article/deadly-force-in-black-and-white#comments. Accessed August 27, 2015.

14. "Investigation of the Ferguson Police Department," United States Department of Justice, Civil Rights Division, March 4, 2015, www .justice.gov/sites/default/files/opa/press-releases/attachments/2015 /03/04/ferguson_police_department_report.pdf. Accessed August 27, 2015.

15. Dylan Matthews, "The Black/White Marijuana Arrest Gap, in Nine Charts," *Washington Post*, June 24, 2013, www.washingtonpost.com/news /wonkblog/wp/2013/06/04/the-blackwhite-marijuana-arrest-gap-in -nine-charts. Accessed August 20, 2015.

16. "'Don't Obey' 'White Man's Law' New Black Panthers: Street Law Says Zimmerman Is Murderer," *Breitbart*, March 29, 2012, www.breitbart .com/video/2012/03/29/dont-obey-white-man-law-new-black-panthers. Accessed August 31, 2015.

17. See Exodus 21:16; Deuteronomy 24:7.

18. See Deuteronomy 15:12-18.

19. Rachel Held Evans, "Repenting of 'Colorblindness,'" blog post, June 26, 2015, http://rachelheldevans.com/blog/repenting-of-colorblindness -charleston-shooting. Accessed August 11, 2015.

20. Marc Fisher, "Cincinnati Still Healing from Its Riots, and Has Lessons to Share with Ferguson," *Washington Post*, September 5, 2014, www .washingtonpost.com/politics/cincinnati-still-healing-from-its-riots -and-has-lessons-to-share-with-ferguson/2014/09/05/2ff8b944-34a1 -11e4-9e92-0899b306bbea_story.html. Accessed August 11, 2015.

CHAPTER 6: SAD AND SYMPATHETIC

1. *A Time to Kill*, directed by Joel Schumacher (1996; Warner Bros., Regency Enterprises).

2. Ibid.

3. Ibid.

4. Dietrich Bonhoeffer, *The Cost of Discipleship* (New York: Touchstone, 1995), 44–45.
5. See Acts 2:38.
6. Psalm 93:4, KJV.
7. "Samuel DuBose's Mother on His Death: 'I Can Forgive,'" press conference, *ABC News*, July 29, 2015, http://abcnews.go.com/US/video /samuel-duboses-mother-death-forgive-32763805.
8. Ibid.

CHAPTER 7: OFFENDED

1. Angelique S. Chengelis, "Michigan's Devin Gardner Beaten, but Not Broken," *Detroit News*, October 21, 2014, www.detroitnews.com/story /sports/college/university-michigan/2014/10/20/michigans-devin -gardner-beaten-broken/17644187/. Accessed August 19, 2015.
2. Chimamanda Ngozi Adichie, "The Danger of a Single Story." Filmed July 2009. TED video, 18:49. Accessed August 19, 2015. www.ted .com/talks/chimamanda_adichie_the_danger_of_a_single_story ?language=en#t-606312.
3. Ibid.
4. Ibid.

CHAPTER 8: HOPELESS

1. Robert F. Kennedy, "Remarks on the Assassination of Martin Luther King Jr.," *Genius*, http://genius.com/1420015/Robert-f-kennedy-remarks-on-the-assassination-of-martin-luther-king-jr/To-tame-the-savageness-of-man -and-make-gentle-the-life-of-this-world. Accessed August 24, 2015.
2. Scott Clement, "Millennials Are Just as Racist as Their Parents," *Washington Post*, June 23, 2015, www.washingtonpost.com/news /wonkblog/wp/2015/06/23/millennials-are-just-as-racist-as-their-parents. Accessed August 20, 2015.
3. "Narrative Change Makes White Supremacy Groups More Dangerous, Expert Says," *NPR Morning Edition*, June 24, 2015, www.npr.org/2015 /06/24/417045112/narrative-change-makes-white-supremacy-groups -more-dangerous-expert-says. Accessed August 20, 2015.
4. Daniel Politi, "Poll: Majority of Americans Are Racist," *Slate*, October 27, 2012, www.slate.com/blogs/the_slatest/2012/10/27/poll_finds_ majority_of_americans_are_racist_prejudiced_against_blacks.html. Accessed August 20, 2015.
5. National Association for the Advancement of Colored People. "Criminal Justice Fact Sheet," www.naacp.org/pages/criminal-justice-fact-sheet. Accessed August 20, 2015.
6. Dylan Matthews, "The Black/White Marijuana Arrest Gap, in Nine Charts," *Washington Post*, June 24, 2013, www.washingtonpost.com/news /wonkblog/wp/2013/06/04/the-blackwhite-marijuana-arrest-gap-in -nine-charts. Accessed August 20, 2015.

7. Alan Noble, "The Naked Racism of an Obama America," *Christ and Pop Culture*, November 19, 2012, http://christandpopculture.com/the -naked-racism-of-an-obama-america. Accessed August 20, 2015.

8. The photo, taken by Johnny H. Nguyen, is featured in Sam Frizell, "A Cop Hugs a Tearful Boy in This Powerful Ferguson Protest Photo," *Time*, November 29, 2014. It can be viewed online at http://time.com /3610385/a-cop-hugs-a-tearful-boy-in-this-powerful-ferguson-protest -photo. Accessed August 26, 2015.

9. Ta-Nehisi Coates, *Between the World and Me* (New York: Spiegel & Grau, 2015), 10.

10. Egberto Willies, "Bill O'Reilly's Guest Believes There Is No Institutional Racism in America," *Daily Kos*, June 24, 2015, www.dailykos.com/story /2015/06/24/1396032/-Bill-O-Reilly-s-guest-believes-there-is-no -institutional-racism-in-America#. Accessed August 26, 2015. See also Scott Eric Kaufman, "'Hannity' panel: There's no such thing as institutional racism in America anymore," *Salon*, June 23, 2015, www .salon.com/2015/06/23/hannity_panel_theres_no_such_thing_as _institutional_racism_in_america_anymore. Accessed August 26, 2015. See also Justin Baragona, "Can White Conservative Pundits Please Stop Saying That Racism Doesn't Exist?" *PoliticusUSA*, April 12, 2014, www .politicususa.com/2014/04/12/white-conservative-pundits-stop-racism -exist.html. Accessed August 26, 2015.

11. Ta-Nehisi Coates, "The Myth of Western Civilization," *The Atlantic*, December 31, 2013, http://www.theatlantic.com/international/archive /2013/12/the-myth-of-western-civilization/282704. Accessed August 21, 2015.

CHAPTER 9: HOPEFUL

1. More of my dad's life story and testimony can be found in Michael V. Fariss, *Reconciling an Oppressor* (Enumclaw, WA: Pleasant Word, 2003).

2. Abigail Thernstrom and Stephan Thernstrom, "Black Progress: How Far We've Come, and How Far We Have to Go," Brookings, March 1, 1998, www.brookings.edu/research/articles/1998/03/spring- affirmativeaction-thernstrom. Accessed September 2, 2015.

3. Ibid.

4. Bill Parcells, enshrinement speech at his induction into the Pro Football Hall of Fame, August 3, 2013, www.profootballhof.com/hof /member.aspx?PlayerId=309&tab=Speech. Accessed September 2, 2015.

CHAPTER 10: ENCOURAGED

1. "Ben Carson: Our Skin Does Not Make Us Who We Are, Our Brain Does," CNSNews.com, August 7, 2015, www.cnsnews.com/news /article/cnsnewscom-staff/ben-carson-our-skin-does-not-make-us -who-we-are-our-brain-does. Accessed September 2, 2015.

CHAPTER 11: EMPOWERED
1. 1 Corinthians 15:33, NASB.
2. Kayla Rinker, "St. Louis Church Works to Bridge Racial Divide," *The Pathway*, June 9, 2015, http://www.mbcpathway.com/2015/06/09/st-louis -church-works-to-bridge-racial-divide. Accessed September 4, 2015.

ABOUT THE AUTHORS

Benjamin Watson is a tight end for the New Orleans Saints, a writer and speaker, and a widely read and followed commentator on social media.

He attended Duke University as a freshman and transferred to the University of Georgia, where he majored in finance. After an all-SEC senior campaign, he was drafted in the first round of the 2004 NFL draft by the New England Patriots. He won a Super Bowl ring in his rookie season and appeared in another Super Bowl following the 2007 season. After a three-year stint with the Cleveland Browns—including a 2010 season in which he led the Browns in receptions, receiving yards, and receiving touchdowns—Watson signed with the Saints in 2013.

Watson serves on the executive committee of the NFL Players Association and is the founder of the nonprofit One More foundation along with his wife, Kirsten. They live in New Orleans with their five children.

Ken Petersen is a veteran of book publishing, having worked for Tyndale House Publishers and Random House/Crown (Water-Brook Multnomah) in various roles as an acquisition director, editor-in-chief, and vice president. He has written numerous books in such genres as memoir, motivation, self-help, and theology, and he has coached a number of authors in writing and publishing. He lives with his wife, Rita, in Colorado Springs, Colorado.

For more resources, visit

UNDEROURSKINBOOK.COM